BE·KNOW·DO

leader to leader
INSTITUTE

Introduced by
Frances Hesselbein
and
General Eric K. Shinseki (USA Ret.)

Foreword by
Richard E. Cavanagh

BE·KNOW·DO

LEADERSHIP
THE ARMY WAY

(Adapted from the Official Army
Leadership Manual)

leader to leader
INSTITUTE

JOSSEY-BASS
A Wiley Imprint
www.josseybass.com

Copyright © 2004 by the Leader to Leader Institute. No protection is claimed in the works of the United States government, as set forth in portions of this book adapted from *Army Leadership*, U.S. Army White Paper, *Training the Force*, Army News Service materials, and Army values.

Published by Jossey-Bass
A Wiley Imprint
989 Market Street, San Francisco, CA 94103-1741   www.josseybass.com

No part of this publication may be reproduced, stored in a retrieval system, or transmitted in any form or by any means, electronic, mechanical, photocopying, recording, scanning, or otherwise, except as permitted under Section 107 or 108 of the 1976 United States Copyright Act, without either the prior written permission of the Publisher, or authorization through payment of the appropriate per-copy fee to the Copyright Clearance Center, Inc., 222 Rosewood Drive, Danvers, MA 01923, phone: 978-750-8400, fax: 978-646-8700, or on the Web at www.copyright.com. Requests to the Publisher for permission should be addressed to the Permissions Department, John Wiley & Sons, Inc., 111 River Street, Hoboken, NJ 07030, phone: 201-748-6011, fax: 201-748-6008, e-mail: permcoordinator@wiley.com.

Jossey-Bass books and products are available through most bookstores. To contact Jossey-Bass directly, call our Customer Care Department within the U.S. at 800-956-7739 or outside the U.S. at 317-572-3986, or fax to 317-572-4002.

Jossey-Bass also publishes its books in a variety of electronic formats. Some content that appears in print may not be available in electronic books.

The boxed material on page 86 and lower page 132 is used by permission of John Wiley & Sons, Inc.

Library of Congress Cataloging-in-Publication Data

Be, know, do : Leadership the Army way : adapted from the
  official Army leadership manual / introduced by Frances
  Hesselbein and Eric K. Shinseki ; foreword by Richard E.
  Cavanagh.
    p. cm.
  "Leader to Leader Institute."
  Includes bibliographical references and index.
  ISBN 0-7879-7083-2 (alk. paper)
    1. Leadership. 2. Command of troops. I. Hesselbein,
  Frances. II. Shinseki, Eric K.
  HD57.7.B4 2004
  658.4'092—dc22

                                        2003026457

Printed in the United States of America
FIRST EDITION
HB Printing   10 9 8 7 6 5 4 3 2 1

About the Leader to Leader Institute

The Leader to Leader Institute has its roots in the social sector and its predecessor, the Peter F. Drucker Foundation for Nonprofit Management, which in January 2003 transferred its ongoing activities to the new identity. The Institute furthers its mission "to strengthen the leadership of the social sector" by providing educational opportunities and resources to leaders.

The Institute serves as a broker of intellectual capital, bringing together the finest thought leaders, consultants, and authors in the world with the leaders of social sector voluntary organizations. By providing intellectual resources to leaders in the business, government, and social sectors, and by fostering partnerships across these sectors, the Leader to Leader Institute works to strengthen social sector leaders of the United States and of nations around the globe.

The Leader to Leader Institute believes that a healthy society requires three vital sectors: a public sector of effective governments, a private sector of effective businesses, and a social sector of effective community organizations. The mission of the social sector is changing lives. It accomplishes this mission by addressing the needs of the spirit, the mind, and the body—of individuals, the community, and society. The social sector also provides a significant sphere for individuals and corporations to practice effective and responsible citizenship.

The Leader to Leader Institute is a 501(c)3 charitable organization. It does not make financial grants. Its offerings fall in three areas:

- Supporting social sector leaders of character and competence

- Forging cross-sector partnerships that deliver social sector results

- Providing leadership resources that engage and inform social sector leaders

Get to Know the Leader to Leader Institute

See leadertoleader.org for information on our programs and articles and resources from *Leader to Leader* journal. Join as a member and support our work.

Contents

Foreword

Three years ago, in the midst of the Internet bubble, our dinner party at the landmark Four Seasons restaurant in Manhattan listened raptly to Peter Drucker, the Father of Modern Management, and Jack Welch, the then widely admired CEO of America's most admired company. The question before us: Who does the best job developing leaders?

To my surprise, the usual suspects so often cited for finding and training leaders didn't figure—not the Harvard Business School, or Goldman Sachs, or McKinsey & Company, or General Electric, or IBM, or Procter & Gamble. The enthusiastic choice of both of these management legends was the United States military.

Military leaders have not always enjoyed the respect they do today. Not so long ago, business leaders and entrepreneurs topped the national poll lists of most respected individuals, and military officers brought up the rear. But today the positions are reversed, partly because of business scandals and excesses, but more importantly because of the quiet, consistent, effective efforts of our leaders in uniform to improve their performance and strengthen their capabilities.

The challenge of leadership for the military, and for the U.S. Army in particular, is exceptional. A massive but progressively smaller force of volunteers, drawn from all of America with some active and some in reserve, employing sophisticated technology, operating anywhere and any time, pursues the single noble mission: "There can be no substitute for victory." And unlike institutions in other sectors, leaders must be developed from within—there are no executive search firms to find generals of competing armies to fill vacancies or strengthen skills.

All this background explains why the civilian adaptation of the Army leadership manual *Be Know Do* is such an exciting development in the field of management. What follows is the extraordinary collaboration of two great leaders—the highly respected and much decorated former Army Chief of Staff Eric Shinseki and his colleague Frances Hesselbein, who has given inspiration first to a generation of Girl Scouts and later to a generation of nonprofit leaders. Their wisdom has been captured, with the help of editor extraordinaire Alan Shrader, in this essential volume.

Both those who lead today and those who aspire to leadership tomorrow have a great deal to learn from the Army's tried-and-true approach—whether they seek to serve business or government or in the independent sector. Leadership is first and foremost a character-based and value-driven art, not just management and communication skills. All leaders, like Shinseki and Hesselbein, are master teachers who share their experience and wisdom, and that of the nation's great creator of leaders, in this action-based book.

Although this book will not answer every question that leaders confront, it will help explain why Drucker and Welch were so right and timely that evening in New York. And those in all walks of life who follow its principles will discover that leadership is an art that can be learned.

January 2004   Richard E. Cavanagh
                                                  President and CEO,
                                                  The Conference Board, Inc.

Introduction

Since we first met five or six years ago, we have collaborated regularly and repeatedly on leadership issues—on the historic battlefield at Gettysburg, at West Point, at Fort Leavenworth, at the Pentagon, and at the Leader to Leader Institute in Manhattan. Though we come from very different backgrounds—one a nonprofit leader, the other a career soldier for thirty-eight years—we have both come to realize, first, that the Army's approach to developing leadership is powerful and eminently successful and, second, that that approach is applicable to institutions and organizations other than the military. With that in mind, we and The Conference Board sponsored conferences that brought together Army, corporate, and nonprofit leaders. One would think that leaders from such varied sectors would not have much in common, but they merged into remarkably cohesive groups. Indeed, there are common denominators among all leaders of quality, and Army leader-development principles capitalize on that fact.

Field Manual 22-100, *Army Leadership,* has three words on its cover: "Be, Know, Do." After reviewing the draft of this Army doctrinal publication on leadership, Frances shared an important insight with a colonel from the Center for Army Leadership at Fort Leavenworth. She said, "Before we review this together, may I say that this manual could be as helpful to the Salvation Army as to the U.S. Army." She realized intuitively that the Army was about to publish a leadership manual that would be as useful to a general, a lieutenant, or a sergeant as to a captain of industry, a mid-level manager, or a front-line customer service representative. "Be, Know, Do" is a great model for all who appreciate the power of language and the ideas that language conveys. The implications of those three words—the demands they make—are profound, far reaching, and relevant to any leader.

All people and all good organizations share the same requirements for strong, selfless leadership. And to develop and institutionalize this kind of leadership, the Army does two things each and every day: it trains its soldiers, and it grows them into leaders. The principles and practices of effective leadership that make the United States Army the greatest landforce in the world are relevant, as well, to civilian organizations—businesses, nonprofit organizations, and governmental agencies. Understanding and accepting the validity of this important proposition prompted the Leader to Leader Institute to compile lessons from the Army and publish them in this book.

Leader Development Is Essential

The American way of life and our well-being depends on the ability of Army leaders at all levels to inspire and lead, often under the most harrowing conditions and unimaginable levels of stress. And the Army has long understood that there is no substitute for strong leaders—throughout its ranks. During combat, squad leaders, platoon leaders, company commanders, and battalion commanders can be incapacitated or killed—as can their replacements and their subordinates. The cost of failure at any point in its complex formations could well be catastrophic, as risks are most often measured in lives. Filling the ranks with well-trained, highly motivated, and performance-oriented soldiers who, without hesitation, can and will step forward to lead when victory hangs in the balance is the unrelenting requirement for success in battle. The Army, therefore, makes leadership everyone's priority.

The Army's record for developing leaders is superb. Today, it is one of the most innovative training organizations in the world. Although many companies in the private sector endorse promoting from within their ranks, contracted executive search firms most often fill top positions by attracting talent from other organizations. This is not an option for the Army; it does not indulge the free agency process. To train and grow effective leaders takes years. And because the Army does not have the luxury of raiding competitors for leadership talent, its top leaders must devote themselves to and succeed in developing new generations of leaders who can cope with uncertainty when preparing for crises yet to be defined. Thus, throughout its history, the Army has found leaders of extraordinary character who have risen to lead the Army and the nation through crisis—Generals Ulysses S. Grant, Robert E. Lee, John J. Pershing, George C. Marshall, Dwight D. Eisenhower, Omar N. Bradley, Creighton W. Abrams, and Colin L. Powell, to name just a few.

Growing Successful Leaders for a Changing Environment

In entering this new century, we have also entered an era of unprecedented change, one that is enormously challenging strategically. Though time-tested leadership practices remain viable, those practices will need to be augmented with new leader competencies that are relevant to the dynamic global environment in which the Army and the nation must prevail decisively. Consider this description of the Objective Force, the vision toward which The Army is working:

> The human dimension of warfare will always remain pre-eminent. War is uncertain, mentally complex, physically demanding, and an intensely emotional experience. Objective Force Soldiers must be physically and mentally tough enough to dominate their opponents despite these challenges. Objective Force Soldiers and leaders

must also possess the competence and confidence to close with their opponents in open, close, and complex terrain—and kill them. They must be highly trained in all tasks across the spectrum of military operations. They must be knowledgeable and disciplined in their application of Rules of Engagement. They must be multifaceted, adaptive, and self-aware—knowing how to clear a room, send a digital message, or repair a vehicle— because sustainment in the first 72 hours of a deployment on a non-linear battlefield will be limited. These Soldiers will need demanding, realistic training conducted by leaders who feel a moral obligation to train them correctly and make them tough, disciplined, and motivated. Knowing and adhering to high standards of discipline, fitness, and competency are essential to Objective Force success ["Concepts for the Objective Force," U.S. Army White Paper].

Physically and mentally tough, competent and confident, highly trained, knowledgeable and disciplined, multifaceted, adaptive, self-aware—these are the characteristics of successful leaders in the twenty-first century. We *can* develop the leaders that our organizations require for an uncertain future, and we believe everyone who aspires to lead or to train leaders can learn from the Army. Since before the birth of the nation and through eras of remarkable change, the Army has been developing leadership principles and practices that speak to the constants of effective leadership—loyalty, duty, respect, selfless service, honor, integrity, and personal courage.

The Army must always be ready to fight and win the wars of the nation—it has this duty as a nonnegotiable contract with the American people. In the wake of the War of 1812, Secretary of War John C. Calhoun described the sole purpose for a peacetime Army—"to prepare for war." To that end, the Army trains to fight every day. And through every period of its more than 228-year history, the

Army has continued to refine its approach to leadership as a matter of embracing relevant change. Since the mid-1970s, the Army has undergone a monumental training revolution. It has refined training doctrine, improved training techniques, raised the bar on performance standards, focused soldiers on individual competence, and focused units on collective performance, all to attain higher levels of warfighting readiness. Army training stresses attainment of competence at individual tasks that are performed repeatedly at increasing levels of difficulty until realistic conditions of combat are most closely simulated. Thus, individual competence becomes the building block for collective team performance of the most complex tasks to the prescribed standard in actual combat. Candid After-Action Reviews (AARs)—a staple of Army leader development—promote and nurture teamwork, strengthen clear communications, emphasize personal accountability, encourage performance to standard, and acknowledge shared risk. The product of AARs is the development of organizational trust and growth in leadership that is effective in any scenario, no matter how the environment may change. This innovative training methodology has been so successful that many of the nation's most renowned corporations have adopted it.

Sharing the Army's Approach with Today's Generation

During World War II and its immediate aftermath, military culture was a familiar part of American life. The Army and its values were integral to our national culture. Millions of Americans in what Tom Brokaw came to call "The Greatest Generation" had fought in World War II, and even those who did not participate directly had fathers, husbands, brothers, and sons—in some cases mothers, wives, sisters, and daughters—who did. They learned about sacrifice, about serving a purpose greater than self, and about determination, teamwork, and trust. While the military draft was in effect, large numbers of men spent two years of their lives in uniform. Their common experiences provided a shared bond, a shared language, and shared values; but the breadth of this experience began to erode early in the 1970s.

Since the end of the draft and the establishment of the all-volunteer force in 1973, fewer and fewer citizens have been exposed to the Army, its values, and its leadership ethos. Today, a smaller segment of the population is familiar with the Army and Army values. A still smaller percentage has participated in Army life and had the chance to benefit from its focus on leaders of character and institutional values. This is unfortunate because the Army continues to provide a premier leadership development opportunity for the nation. How does it do it? How can we use the principles of Army Leadership to strengthen other parts of our society, of our corporate, governmental, or nonprofit organizations? Exploring and answering those questions is the Leader to Leader Institute's purpose in this book.

All Leaders Can Benefit

Leadership matters. It matters in the life and death situations in which a lack of trust, teamwork, clear focus, confidence, and motivation could spell disaster—leadership matters in combat. Leadership matters when preparing soldiers for the rigors of combat in realistic training scenarios that simulate combat with inherently dangerous equipment and munitions. And leadership matters during the down time, as well, when soldiers prepare for future missions, plan training, repair and maintain equipment, and spend time with their families. Leadership of successful organizations is not a nine-to-five, five-day-a-week duty. It is a way of life. It underscores every organizational endeavor. Consider that, while advances in materials and technology have changed the face of battle, the Army continues to rely most heavily on strong leaders at all levels— exceptional leaders who are self-aware, adaptive, and agile; leaders who will hold units together in the midst of tragedy; leaders who will achieve their objectives in the face of concerted opposition and the most overwhelming odds. These are leaders of indomitable spirit who fulfill their obligations to their assigned missions and to their people. Soldier-leaders represent what's best about the Army. They deliver our magnificent moments—noble by sacrifice, magnificent by performance, and respected by all. They make us better than we ever expected to be.

In the post-9/11 world, leaders in all organizations can gain from the Army's approach to leadership. Even if we don't face the life and death challenges of combat, civilian leaders do face unprecedented change, ruthless competition, unexpected threats, and battles for market share—all of which can mean the survival or destruction of products, careers, and companies and can have serious consequences for the people who are the heart and soul of all institutions.

In this book, the Leader to Leader Institute shares the Army's leadership philosophy with leaders from many sectors—business, government, nonprofits, and volunteer organizations. It adapts material from the Army's primary leadership manual, *Army Leadership*, and draws lessons from Army leaders at a variety of levels and across its formations. It offers practical advice to leaders everywhere on how to use Army leadership principles to transform themselves and their organizations into more effective, efficient, and committed teams that work toward common goals. We know firsthand the challenges leaders face, and we have learned how well the Army prepares its people to meet them.

Leadership is most important when the stakes are highest, but it must be continuously developed, patiently nurtured, and tested with uncertainty if it is to be fully ready for those unforeseen crises. In today's turbulent world, Army leadership is being tested daily around the globe in battles that were not envisioned three years ago, and the Army is meeting every challenge.

January 2004   Frances Hesselbein

General Eric K. Shinseki,
United States Army (Retired)

WHAT A LEADER MUST BE, KNOW, AND DO

Just Calm Down or None of Us Will Get Back Alive

"Sarge" was a company favorite, a big powerful kid from New Jersey who talked with his hands and played up his "Joy-zee" accent. He loved practical jokes. One of his favorites was to put those tiny charges in guys' cigarettes, the kind that would explode with a loud *pop!* about halfway through a smoke. If anyone else had done it, it would have been annoying; Sarge usually got everyone to laugh— even the guy whose cigarette he destroyed.

During the October 3, 1993, raid in Mogadishu, Sarge was manning his Humvee's .50 cal when he was hit and killed. The driver and some of the guys in back screamed, "He's dead! He's dead!" They panicked and were not responding as their squad leader tried to get someone else up and behind the gun. The squad leader had to yell at them, "Just calm down! We've got to keep fighting or none of us will get back alive."

Consider carefully what the squad leader did. First, he told his squad to calm down. Then he told them why it was important: they had to continue the fight if they wanted to make it back to their base alive. In this way he jerked his soldiers back to a conditioned response, one that had been drilled during training and took their minds off the loss. The squad leader demonstrated the calm, reasoned leadership under stress that's critical to mission success. In spite of the loss, the unit persevered.[1]

How Do You Exercise Enormous Power?

Philip J. Carroll, Jr. joined Fluor Corporation as chief executive officer in July 1998. In a June 1999 interview with Kathye A. Johnson
of the Wharton Executive MBA Program, he recounted how his
experience in the military had shaped his approach to leadership:

> When I was young (high school, college, and postcol-
> lege) I always had an association with the military. The
> high school that I went to had mandatory participation
> in the Marine Corps. I went through ROTC and re-
> ceived a commission in college, served in the Army, and
> then served in the reserves for a number of years. . . .
> The military is a tremendous place for the development
> of leadership characteristics.
>
> It taught me a lot about motivating people and main-
> taining discipline, but not in an oppressive way. That's a
> very important lesson in leadership, because in the mil-
> itary you have absolute power, for the most part. You are
> governed by regulation and when you tell subordinates
> to do something in the form of a direct order, they *have
> to* obey by the laws of the military. Having that enor-
> mous power, particularly as a very young person, how do
> you exercise that? Do you run around giving people a
> bunch of orders, or do you recognize that approach is
> very poor in terms of your long-term ability to make a
> unit function in very difficult circumstances?[2]

---

*"We have recommitted ourselves to doing two things
well each and every day—train soldiers, grow them
into leaders. Those two things. That is the rhythm of
the Army."*

General Eric K. Shinseki (USA Ret.)

If you volunteer in a community organization, work in a large corporation, own a small business, or engage in public service, you have the opportunity to lead. How do you prepare yourself? How do you learn and embrace those values and skills that will enable you to meet the challenge? These are issues that the U.S. Army takes very seriously. The Army works hard to help everyone serving in it to become effective leaders, from the raw recruits in boot camp to the colonels at the Army War College and the generals in major commands around the world. The Army has a proud tradition of leadership, and it works constantly to refine and update its approach to leadership and the methods it uses to teach leadership.

"The Army has a system of values that people in the corporate world would die for," says Dr. James Crupi, a leadership consultant who has worked extensively in corporate and military settings. And one of the highest values is leadership. "Leadership development is much more systematic, much more of a priority in the Army than in the corporate world," he continues. "What is called leadership development in the corporate sector is often really business development, working on business processes, improving financial management or strategic planning. The corporate sector views personal development as somewhat soft. And there is almost a sense in the private sector that you're either a leader or you're not. We'll spend some time on you, we'll invest in you, but really it's all about whether you have it or not. The Army spends a lot of time and investment to make sure it has the leaders it needs, and it's not afraid to do that." Crupi adds, "In the corporate sector, they are much more likely to go out and hire the leaders they need than to development them inside."[3]

According to Patrick Townsend and Joan Gebhardt, authors of *Five-Star Leadership*, "The military has long known that it cannot settle for a random selection process for its leaders. Waiting for leaders to develop naturally is out of the question when the penalty for error is swift and permanent, as it is in combat. . . . To ensure a continuous supply of leaders, leadership training is an ongoing part of the military experience."[4]

Telling Versus Leading

This emphasis on leadership may surprise some who still view the Army through the old stereotype of the "command-and-control" organization. Why bother with leadership when you can just tell people what to do, when you can just give an order (which people have to obey, as Philip Carroll, president of Fluor, pointed out)? To understand the difference between telling people what to do (giving an order) and leadership, consider this simple scenario, played out thousands of times every day in organizations across the country.

You are a manager working on an important deal with a potential customer and have a complex set of documents that need to go out immediately. You take the documents down to the mailroom and hand them to the clerk. "Joe, you have to get these packed up and ready to go by the 4 P.M. express pickup. Send them priority overnight." Seems simple, right? You are a manager and Joe is a mail clerk. You tell him what to do and expect him to comply. Doesn't seem like much leadership is required. You leave and assume that the documents will go out on time and be in the hands of your important future customer early the next day.

But consider what happens next. Jane, a manager at about your level in the company, comes to the mailroom some ten minutes later with a big box of documents. "Joe," she says, "I really need your help on this project. I have an important customer who needs to get these bright and early tomorrow morning. I've been nurturing this relationship for three months and think they'll be really jazzed with what I've been able to put together in this presentation. It will be a big help to me if you can get everything put together and packaged professionally. I know there is a lot of paper here to collate, but it's very important that they get this tomorrow morning. The company is counting on this contract. Can you have this all ready by today's 4 P.M. pickup?"

"Well, I'm pretty backed up right now," Joe replies.

"It's really important, Joe," Jane explains. "You know I don't like to dump stuff on you at the last minute like this, but I really need a favor this time. I can try to find someone to help you out, if you like."

"Well, I think I can manage."

"Call me if you need help."

Now, if Joe does get backed up, whose package do you think will make the 4 P.M. pickup, yours or Jane's? Jane didn't just tell Joe what to do, she explained the situation, why it was important to her and the company, offered help if needed, and asked Joe to follow her willingly. You, on the other hand, simply told Joe what to do.

As this simple example demonstrates, leadership can make a difference in even the most mundane situations. Think how much more important leadership is in more complex and more difficult situations, where it may be uncertain what the facts are, where unexpected obstacles may pop up suddenly, and where the stakes can be enormous, as they are in war. Leadership becomes critical. People need to do more than they are told; they need to participate actively and willingly. They need to be committed to achieving a common objective. Orders and commands don't plant the seeds of commitment; leadership does.

Leadership experts James Kouzes and Barry Posner explain: "Authority and credible leadership aren't the same thing. Doing something willingly because you respect and trust someone is very different from doing something because they have authority to give you an order. Leadership isn't about position; it's about behavior."[5] General of the Army and later President Dwight D. Eisenhower said that a leader "gets his men to go along with him because they want to do it for him and they believe in him. You do not lead by hitting people over the head. Any damn fool can do that, but it's usually called assault, and not leadership. . . . I'll tell you what leadership is. It's persuasion, and conciliation and education and patience."[6]

Army Leadership, the Army's official leadership manual, defines leadership this way: "Leadership is influencing people—by providing purpose, direction, and motivation—while operating to accomplish the mission and improving the organization." There's not a word about issuing orders in a commanding voice. "Leadership transforms human potential into effective performance," according to Army doctrine.

Leadership at Every Level

In the stereotypical view of the military organization, a few people at the top give commands, and everyone down the line salutes and does what he or she is told. But if this old picture were ever true, it is certainly *not* true today. Consider just who in the Army is expected to be a leader, according to the Army's leadership manual. It's not just generals:

> At any level, anyone responsible for supervising people or accomplishing a mission that involves other people is a leader. Anyone who influences others, motivating them to action or influencing their thinking or decision making, is a leader. It's not a function only of position; it's also a function of role. In addition, everyone in the Army—including every leader—fits somewhere in a chain of command. Everyone in the Army is also a follower or subordinate. There are, obviously, many leaders in an organization, and it's important to understand that you don't just lead subordinates—you lead other leaders. Even at the lowest level, you are a leader of leaders.

Think of that: "Even at the lowest level, you are a leader of leaders." This is about as far from command-and-control as it gets.

D-Day, 1944, provides a good illustration of the importance of developing leadership at all organizational levels. As told in the Army's leadership manual, the amphibious landings on the beaches of Normandy were preceded by a nighttime parachute assault by American and British airborne units. Many of the thousands of aircraft that delivered the 82nd and 101st U.S. Airborne Divisions to Normandy were blown off-course. Some wound up in the wrong place because of enemy fire; others were simply lost. Thousands of paratroopers, the spearhead of the Allied invasion of Western Europe, found themselves scattered across unfamiliar countryside, many of them miles from their drop zones. They wandered about in the night, searching for their units, their buddies, their leaders, and their objectives. The fate of the invasion hung in the balance; if the paratroopers did not cut the roads leading to the beaches, the Germans could counterattack the landing forces at the water's edge, crushing the invasion before it even began.

Fortunately for the Allies and for the soldiers in the landing craft, the leaders of these airborne forces had trained their subordinate leaders well, encouraging their initiative, allowing them to do their jobs. Small unit leaders who were scattered around the darkened, unfamiliar countryside knew they were part of a larger effort, and they knew its success was up to them. They had been trained to act instead of waiting to be told what to do; they knew that if the invasion was to succeed, their small units had to accomplish their individual missions.

Among these leaders were men like Captain Sam Gibbons of the 505th Parachute Infantry Regiment. He gathered a group of twelve soldiers from different commands—people he had never seen before—and liberated a tiny village, which turned out to be outside the division area of operations, before heading south toward his original objective, the Douve River bridges nearly fifteen kilometers away. Later he remarked, "This certainly wasn't the way I had thought the invasion would go, nor had we ever rehearsed it in this manner." But he was moving out to accomplish the mission. Throughout the area, small unit leaders were doing the same.

This was the payoff for leaders who valued soldiers, communicated the importance of the mission, and trusted their subordinate leaders to accomplish it. Because they knew their units were well trained and their leaders would do everything in their power to support them, small unit leaders were able to focus on the force's overall mission. They knew and understood the commander's intent. They believed that if they exercised disciplined initiative within that intent, things would turn out. And they were right. D-Day was a success because of leadership at every level. Soldiers followed commands, of course, but they didn't just follow commands. They did much, much more.

John Gardner, former Secretary of Health, Education, and Welfare, put it this way: "We are dependent on leaders at many levels and in all segments of our society—business, government, organized labor, agriculture, the professions, the minority communities, the arts, the universities, social agencies, and so on. They are city councilmen and school superintendents, factory managers and editors, heads of local unions and heads of social agencies, lawyers, and health commissioners. If it weren't for this wide dispersal of leadership, our kind of society couldn't function. Excessive dependence on central definition and rule-making produces standardized solutions to be applied uniformly throughout the system. But the world 'out there,' the world to be coped with, isn't standardized. It is diverse, localized, and surprising."[7]

In a world that is more "diverse, localized, and surprising" than ever before, leadership has to be everyone's job. There is no alternative.

Three Components of Leadership

There are three aspects to leadership regardless of organizational level or military rank: who you are inside, what you know, and how you act. The Army encapsulates leadership at all levels by focusing on three simple yet powerful words: *Be, Know, Do*. Can three little words really sum up all the tangible and intangible qualities of leadership? Let's look at what the Army leadership manual says.

Be

What does "Be" have to do with leadership?

Leadership starts at the top, with the character of the leader, with *your* character. In order to lead others, you must first make sure your own house is in order. For example, the first line of the Creed of the Noncommissioned Officer states, "No one is more professional than I." But it takes a remarkable person to move from memorizing a creed to actually living that creed; a true leader *is* that remarkable person.

Army leadership begins with what the leader must *Be*, the values and attributes that shape a leader's character. It may be helpful to think of these as internal qualities: you possess them all the time, when you're alone and when you're with others. They define who you are; they give you a solid footing. These values and attributes are the same for all leaders, regardless of position, although you certainly refine your understanding of them as you become more experienced and assume positions of greater responsibility. For example, a sergeant major with combat experience has a deeper understanding of selfless service and personal courage than a new soldier does.

The kind of person you are as a leader is critically important. In their research on leadership reported in *The Leadership Challenge*, James Kouzes and Barry Posner surveyed thousands of people in business and government, asking an open-ended question: "What values (personal traits or characteristics) do you look for and admire in your leader?" And they define a leader as someone you would willingly follow. "The key word . . . is willingly. What do they expect from a leader they would follow not because they *have to*, but because they *want to*?"[8] Over two decades of asking this question in the United States and around the world, Kouzes and Posner say the results are remarkably consistent. People want leaders who are:

- Honest

- Competent

- Forward-looking

- Inspiring

Think of yourself. Would you *want to* follow anyone who did not radiate these qualities? David Pottruck, president and co-CEO of

Charles Schwab says, "Virtually everyone I've ever met wanted to work with people of impeccable character."[9]

Philip J. Carroll, whom we quoted at the beginning of this chapter, talks about consistency and authenticity as part of what the leader must be: "Some people fail in leadership because you never know from day to day how they're going to act. It's not just temporal inconsistency but the worst thing of all is to have inconsistency of behavior or action in terms of hierarchy. That is, you act a certain way with a certain group of people and then you act a different way with a different group of people and then you act a different way when you're out on a project. You have to have that consistency across the people with whom you deal and consistency over time. There is another way of describing that, and that is *authenticity*."

The great General of the Army George C. Marshall, speaking to officer candidates on the eve of World War II, commented on the importance of being a leader of character: "When you are commanding, leading [soldiers] under conditions where physical exhaustion and privations must be ignored, where the lives of [soldiers] may be sacrificed, then the efficiency of your leadership will depend only to a minor degree on your tactical ability. It will primarily be determined by your character, your reputation, not so much for courage—which will be accepted as a matter of course—but by the previous reputation you have established for fairness, for that high-minded patriotic purpose, that quality of unswerving determination to carry through any military task assigned to you."[10] For more on what it means to *Be* a leader, see Exhibit 1.1.

Know

Let's look now at the second word in the *Be, Know, Do* trilogy. "The American soldier . . . demands professional competence in his leaders," General Omar Bradley said. And this is true not only in the Army but everywhere in the public, private, and nonprofit sectors. People willingly follow only those who know what they are doing. One of the quickest ways for a leader to lose the trust and commitment of followers is to demonstrate incompetence. This does not

Exhibit 1.1. Be

Character describes a person's inner strength, the *Be* of *Be, Know, Do*. Your character helps you know what is right; more than that, it links that knowledge to action. Character gives you the courage to do what is right regardless of the circumstances or the consequences.

You demonstrate character through your behavior. One of your key responsibilities as a leader is to teach Army values to your subordinates. The old saying that actions speak louder than words has never been more true than here. Leaders who talk about honor, loyalty, and selfless service but do not live these values—both on- and off-duty—send the wrong message, that this "values stuff" is all just talk.

Here are the Army values that guide you, the leader, and the rest of the Army. They form the acronym LDRSHIP:

- Loyalty
- Duty
- Respect
- Selfless service
- Honor
- Integrity
- Personal courage

Values tell us part of what the leader must *Be*; the other side of what a leader must *Be* are the attributes listed above. Leader attributes influence leader actions; leader actions, in turn, always influence the unit or organization. As an example, if you're physically fit, you're more likely to inspire your subordinates to be physically fit. The mental attributes of an Army leader include will, self-discipline, initiative, judgment, self-confidence, intelligence, and cultural awareness. Physical attributes—health and physical fitness, military and professional bearing—can be developed. Army leaders maintain the appropriate level of physical fitness and military bearing.

As an Army leader, your emotional attributes—self-control, balance, and stability—contribute to how you feel and therefore to how you interact with others. Your people are human beings with hopes, fears, concerns, and dreams. When you understand that will and endurance come from emotional energy, you possess a powerful leadership tool. The feedback you give can help your subordinates use their emotional energy to accomplish amazing feats in tough times. Self-control, balance, and stability also help you make the right ethical choices.

Understanding Army values and leader attributes is only the first step. You also must embrace Army values and develop leader attributes, living them until they become habit. You must teach Army values to your subordinates through action and example and help them develop leader attributes in themselves.

mean that the leader must have all the answers. Far from it. It does mean that the leader must have a certain level of knowledge and mastery of four key skills.

- *Interpersonal skills* include coaching, teaching, counseling, motivating, and empowering individuals, as well as building teams.

- *Conceptual skills* include the ability to think creatively and to reason analytically, critically, and ethically, which are the bases of sound judgment.

- *Technical skills* are job-related abilities. They include the expertise necessary to accomplish all tasks and functions within a leader's responsibility.

- *Tactical skills* in the military apply to solving problems concerning employment of units in combat to achieve an objective. In civilian life, tactical skills involving negotiation, human relations, budgeting, and the like are often necessary to achieve objectives.

Good leaders make it a regular practice to add to their knowledge and skills. They seek out mentors, opportunities to learn, and challenges that will force them to grow. For a closer look at the Army's approach to what a leader must *Know*, see Exhibit 1.2.

Do

Character and competence, the *Be* and the *Know*, underlie everything a leader does. But character and knowledge—while absolutely necessary—are not enough. Leaders act; they *Do*. They bring together everything they are, everything they believe, and everything they know how to do to provide purpose, direction, and motivation. Leaders in the Army and civilian organizations alike work to influence people, operate to accomplish the mission, and act to improve their organization. They solve problems, overcome obstacles, strengthen

Exhibit 1.2. Know

Leaders in combat combine interpersonal, conceptual, technical, and tactical skills to accomplish the mission. They use their interpersonal skills to communicate their intent effectively and motivate their soldiers. They apply their conceptual skills to determine viable concepts of operations, make the right decisions, and execute the tactics the operational environment requires. They capitalize on their technical skills to properly employ the techniques, procedures, fieldcraft, and equipment that fit the situation. Finally, combat leaders employ tactical skill, combining skills from the other skill categories with knowledge of the art of tactics appropriate to their level of responsibility and unit type to accomplish the mission. When plans go wrong and leadership must turn the tide, it is tactical skill, combined with character, that enables an Army leader to seize control of the situation and lead the unit to mission accomplishment.

The Army leadership framework draws a distinction between developing skills and performing actions. Army leaders who take their units to a combat training center (CTC) improve their skills by performing actions—by doing their jobs on the ground in the midst of intense simulated combat. But they don't wait until they arrive at the CTC to develop their skills; they practice ahead of time in command-post exercises, in combat drills, on firing ranges, and even on the physical training (PT) field.

Your leader skills will improve as your experience broadens. A platoon sergeant gains valuable experience on the job that will help him be a better first sergeant. Army leaders take advantage of every chance to improve: they look for new learning opportunities, ask questions, seek training opportunities, and request performance critiques.

Mastery of different skills in these domains is essential to the Army's success in peace and war. But a true leader is not satisfied with knowing only how to do what will get the organization through today; you must also be concerned about what it will need tomorrow. You must strive to master your job and prepare to take over your boss's job. In addition, as you move to jobs of increasing responsibility, you'll face new equipment, new ideas, and new ways of thinking and doing things. You must learn to apply all these to accomplish your mission.

---

teamwork, and achieve objectives. They use leadership to produce results.

Leaders also take deliberate action to develop all aspects of themselves. In the Army, this includes adopting and living Army values. But in every setting, leaders need to have clear values and live those values. Only with this self-development does a person become a confident and competent leader of character. Being a leader is not easy, especially in the Army. There are no cookie-cutter solutions to leadership challenges, and there are no shortcuts to success. However, the tools are available to every leader. It is up to each individual to master and use them.

Successful leaders act in three key ways: they pull people together in teams and organizations with a unified purpose, they execute to achieve results, and they lead change to leave the organization stronger than they found it. In the Army's language, these three areas of action are called influencing, operating, and improving.

- *Influencing:* Leaders use interpersonal skills to guide others toward a goal. Influencing includes making decisions, communicating those decisions clearly, and motivating people to act in accordance with those decisions. Direct, or frontline, leaders most often influence subordinates face-to-face—such as when a team leader gives instructions, recognizes achievement, and encourages hard work. Organizational and strategic leaders also influence their immediate subordinates and staff face-to-face; however, they guide their organizations primarily by indirect influence. At all levels, influence is critical in building teams and promoting teamwork.

- *Operating:* Leaders act to accomplish their organization's immediate mission and objectives. They develop detailed, executable plans and execute those plans, take care of their people, and effectively manage their resources. And they assess the efficiency and effectiveness of their own and their organization's actions so they can determine what needs to be done to sustain the strong areas and improve weak ones. This kind of forward thinking is linked to the last leader action: improving.

- *Improving:* Good leaders strive to leave an organization in better shape than they found it, taking steps
  to increase its capability to accomplish current or
  future missions. All leaders are tempted to focus on
  the short-term gain that makes them and their organizations look good today: "Why bother to fix it now?
  By the time next year rolls around, it will be someone
  else's problem." Leaders who are loyal to their people
  and the larger organization consider the long-term
  effects of their actions. They invest adequate time
  and effort to develop individual subordinates as leaders,
  improve teams, groups, and units, and foster an ethical
  climate. They focus on learning, seeking self-improvement and organizational growth. They are proactive
  in envisioning, adapting, and leading change.

A long-term focus on improving the organization does not mean
demanding perfection; on the contrary, an excellent leader allows
subordinates room to learn from their mistakes as well as from their
successes. In such a climate, people work to improve and take the
risks necessary to learn. They know that when they fall short—as
they will—their leader will seek to understand the reason, give
them new or more detailed instructions, and send them on their
way again.

Competent, confident leaders tolerate honest mistakes that are
not the result of negligence. A leader who sets a standard of "zero
defects, no mistakes" is also saying, "Don't take any chances. Don't
try anything you can't already do perfectly, and for heaven's sake,
don't try anything new." That organization will not improve; in fact,
its ability to perform the mission will deteriorate rapidly.

Sometimes leaders fail to act because of indecision. Indecision
can be fatal on the battlefield, and can lead to failure in other settings. According to Sam Manoogian, who has many years of experience working with leaders at the Center for Creative Leadership

and as an executive coach, "One of the key reasons why executives cannot fully and completely resolve problematic issues is they are not sure what, or who, to believe, or what they really believe they should do." Manoogian says: "The harsh reality is that [difficult issues] probably won't get any easier the longer you wait and it is just wishful thinking to expect a difficult issue to resolve itself. My advice is not to believe the people who say to put off making a decision until as late as possible."

When a problem becomes so difficult that the way ahead seems unclear, it is time to get to work. Manoogian continues, "Solving a difficult issue means really digging into the details—otherwise you would have already addressed it—understanding it more fully, and distilling it down to even more manageable parts. It probably also means you will need to engage others who are either impacted by it or have ideas and suggestions as to what you might do about it. Then you must make the difficult choices and decisions that are necessary."[11]

In the Army, training and preparation are the key tools leaders rely on to prevent paralysis in the face of difficult situations in combat. Training for warfighting is the Army's first priority in peace and in war. As the Army manual *Training the Force* states, "Leader Development is the deliberate, continuous, sequential, and progressive process, based on Army values, that develops soldiers and civilians into competent and confident leaders capable of decisive action." Exhibit 1.3 explains the role of training and leadership development in today's Army.

As with leader skills, leader actions increase in scope and complexity as people move from direct leader positions to organizational and strategic leader positions. Leaders who live up to the highest values, who display leader attributes, who are competent, who act at all times as they would have their people act, will succeed. Leaders who talk a good game but don't back their words with actions will fail in the end.

Exhibit 1.3. Learning to Do

Every soldier, noncommissioned officer (NCO), warrant officer, and officer has one primary mission—to be trained and ready to fight and win our Nation's wars. Success in battle does not happen by accident; it is a direct result of tough, realistic, and challenging training. The Army exists to deter war, or if deterrence fails, to reestablish peace through victory in combat wherever U.S. interests are challenged. To accomplish this, the Army's forces must be able to perform their assigned strategic, operational, and tactical missions. For deterrence to be effective, potential enemies must know with certainty that the Army has the credible, demonstrable capability to mobilize, deploy, fight, sustain, and win any conflict. Training is the process that melds human and materiel resources into these required capabilities. The Army has an obligation to the American people to ensure its soldiers go into battle with the assurance of success and survival. This is an obligation that only rigorous and realistic training, conducted to standard, can fulfill.

We train the way we fight because our historical experiences show the direct correlation between realistic training and success on the battlefield. Today's leaders must apply the lessons of history in planning training for tomorrow's battles. We can trace the connection between training and success in battle to our Army's earliest experiences during the American Revolution. General Washington had long sensed the need for uniform training and organization and, during the winter of 1777–78 while camped at Valley Forge, he secured the appointment of Von Steuben, a Prussian, as inspector general in charge of training. Von Steuben clearly understood the difference between the American citizen-soldier and the European professional. He noted early that American soldiers had to be told why they did things before they would do them well, and he applied this philosophy in his training. It helped the Continental soldiers understand and endure the rigorous and demanding training he put them through. After Valley Forge, Continentals would fight on equal terms with British Regulars. Von Steuben began the tradition of effective unit-level training that today still develops leaders and forges battle-ready units for the Army.

Over two centuries later, the correlation between tough, realistic training and success on the battlefield remains the same. During Operation Enduring Freedom, and Operation Anaconda in Afghanistan, the U.S. Army deployed a trained and ready force on short notice to a contemporary battlefield fighting against a coalition of rebel forces on difficult terrain.

These units trained to their wartime mission, and developed company grade officers, NCOs, and soldiers who knew their jobs and were confident they could act boldly and decisively. Their confidence and technical and tactical competence gave them the ability to adapt to the mission and harsh environment with resounding success. Airmobile infantry quickly perfected methods of routing rebel forces from heavily fortified caves. Special forces teams rode horses with their host nation counterparts—learning to call in tactical air support with devastating accuracy while on the move. Staffs quickly learned how to integrate Special Operations

Exhibit 1.3. Learning to Do, Cont'd

Forces (SOF) and conventional force operations. Engineer units cleared mine fields that were as old as many of their soldiers involved in the clearing process. Again, American soldiers had met the enemy and decisively defeated them.

The Army's battle-focused training was validated. These soldiers trained as they planned to fight and won. Their success was due to the Army's emphasis on battle-focused training, which emphasized training essential warfighting tasks to standard and building cohesive combined arms teams able to adapt to the mission. Army units today train, alert, and deploy prepared for combat. Their battle-focused training experience gives them the flexibility to continue training and adapting to the mission as it evolves.

Leader development is the deliberate, continuous, sequential, and progressive process, grounded in Army values, that grows soldiers and civilians into competent and confident leaders capable of decisive action. Leader development is achieved through the lifelong synthesis of the knowledge, skills, and experiences gained through institutional training and education, organizational training, operational experience, and self-development. Commanders play the key role in leader development that ideally produces tactically and technically competent, confident, and adaptive leaders who act with boldness and initiative in dynamic, complex situations to execute mission-type orders achieving the commander's intent.

Source: Training the Force, Field Manual 7-0.

Leaders Also Follow

Before people can lead, they must learn how to follow. And being a good follower does not just mean passively doing what you are told. In the Army, it means accepting an order and actively carrying it out, overcoming obstacles, solving problems, thinking creatively, finding resources, and carrying through until the objective is achieved.

No one is only a leader; each person in an organization is also a follower and part of a team. In fact, the old distinction between leaders and followers has blurred; complex twenty-first-century organizations require individuals to move seamlessly from one role to another in an organization, from leadership to "followership," and back again.

Part of being a good subordinate is supporting organizational leaders. It's a leader's responsibility to make sure his or her team supports the larger organization. Consider Barbara, a leader whose team is responsible for handling the payroll administration of a large organization. Barbara knows that when the team makes a mistake or falls behind in its work, its customers pay the price in terms of late-pay actions. One day a message from Barbara's boss introducing a new computer system for handling payroll changes arrives. She looks hard at the new system and decides it will not work as well as the old one. The team will spend a lot of time installing the new system, all the while keeping up with their regular workload. Then they'll have to spend more time undoing the work once the new system fails. And Barbara believes it will fail—all her experience points to that.

But Barbara cannot simply say, "We'll let these actions pile up; that'll send a signal to top management about just how bad the new system is and how important we are down here." The team does not exist in a vacuum; it's part of a larger organization. For the good of the organization and the people in it, Barbara, as team leader, must make sure the job gets done.

Because Barbara disagrees with the boss's order and because it affects both the team's mission and the welfare of its members, she must tell the boss; she must have the moral courage to make her opinions known. Of course, Barbara must also have the right attitude; disagreement doesn't mean it's OK to be disrespectful. She must choose the time and place—usually in private—to explain her concerns to the boss fully and clearly. In addition, she must go into the meeting knowing that, at some point, the discussion will be over and she must execute the boss's decision, whatever it is.

Once the boss has listened to all the arguments and made a decision, Barbara must support that decision as if it were her own. If she goes to the team and says, "I still don't think this is a good idea, but we're going to do it anyway," she undermines the chain of command

and teaches her people a bad lesson. Imagine what it would do to an organization's effectiveness if subordinates chose which orders to pursue vigorously and which ones to sleepwalk through. Such an action would also damage Barbara's ability to lead her team: in the future the team may treat her decisions as she treated her boss's. And there is no great leap from people thinking that their leader is disloyal to the boss to thinking that their leader will be disloyal to them as well. The good leader executes the boss's decision with energy and enthusiasm; looking at their leader, subordinates will believe the leader thinks it's absolutely the best possible solution.

Good leaders are loyal to their superiors *and* their subordinates—it is a two-way street. Consider the words of General Edward C. Meyer, former Army Chief of Staff: "When I became Chief of Staff, I set two personal goals for myself. The first was to ensure that the Army was continually prepared to go to war, and the second was to create a climate in which each member could find personal meaning and fulfillment. It is my belief that only by attainment of the second goal will we ensure the first."[12] General Meyer's words make it clear that, in the Army, leaders must accomplish the mission and take care of their soldiers. General Meyer knew that the only way to accomplish the huge goal of preparation was to pay attention to the smallest parts of the organization, the individual soldiers and civilians. Through his subordinate leaders, the General offered challenges and guidance and set the example so that every member of the Army felt a part of the team and knew that the team was doing important work. What is true in the Army is no less true in civilian organizations.

Excellent leaders make certain that all subordinates know the important roles they play. Leaders look for everyday examples that occur under ordinary circumstances: the way a soldier digs a fighting position, prepares for guard duty, fixes a radio, lays an artillery battery; the way a civilian handles an action, takes care of customers, meets a deadline on short notice. Good leaders know that each of these people is contributing in a small but important way to the organization.

Lessons for Civilian Organizations

In a time of ambiguity and anxiety, it seems everything is in a state of flux. Yet the Army's approach to leadership remains constant, and rightly so. Our observations of great leaders and our own work as chief executives have led us to two conclusions. First, leadership is the ability to manage for the organization's mission and mobilize people around that mission. Second, while strategy and tactics change all the time, the fundaments of leadership do not. *Leadership is a matter of how to be, not how to do.* We spend most of our lives mastering how to do things, but in the end it is the quality and character of the individual that distinguishes the great leaders.

In a world where no individual can possibly have all the answers, it is the inclusive organization that excels. Leaders of those organizations know they must disperse leadership across the organization, ban the hierarchy, and create more circular, flexible, and fluid management systems based on collaborative relationships, the wise use of teams, and mutual respect. Today, many organizations claim to have flattened the hierarchy and empowered employees; they claim to have gone beyond command-and-control to make leadership everyone's job. But in our experience, there is a large amount of wishful thinking in these claims. Too many organizations are still ruled by Standing Operating Procedures. Too many people are punished for telling uncomfortable truths. Take a look at your own organization: Does it do too much telling and too little leading? How about your own style? Do you feel too rushed to explain, influence, and motivate? Then you are probably not leading, you are just telling. Organizations, especially large organizations, tend toward command-and-control, but the best recognize the tendency and work deliberately to counteract it, as the Army does.

In the Army, training and leadership development are not line items on the budget to be cut when times get tough. They are essential to the organization and a large part of every leader's job. No matter what your title, no matter how many people report to you, you are not leading if you are not working constantly to help your people develop. In addition, as the Army's leadership manual reminds us, you also need to focus squarely on your own development.

THE CHARACTER
OF LEADERS

When Character Counts Most

During a raid in Mogadishu in October 1993, MSG Gary Gordon and SFC Randall Shughart, leader and member of a sniper team with Task Force Ranger in Somalia, were providing precision and suppressive fires from helicopters above two helicopter crash sites. Learning that no ground forces were available to rescue one of the downed aircrews and aware that a growing number of enemy were closing in on the site, MSG Gordon and SFC Shughart volunteered to be inserted to protect their critically wounded comrades. Their initial request was turned down because of the danger of the situation. They asked a second time; permission was denied. Only after their third request were they inserted.

MSG Gordon and SFC Shughart were inserted one hundred meters south of the downed chopper. Armed only with their personal weapons, the two NCOs fought their way to the downed fliers through intense small-arms fire, a maze of shanties and shacks, and the enemy converging on the site. After MSG Gordon and SFC Shughart pulled the wounded from the wreckage, they established a perimeter, put themselves in the most dangerous position, and fought off a series of attacks. The two NCOs continued to protect their comrades until they had depleted their ammunition and were themselves fatally wounded. Their actions saved the life of an Army pilot.

No one will ever know what was running through the minds of MSG Gordon and SFC Shughart as they left the relative safety of their helicopter to go to the aid of the downed aircrew. The two NCOs knew there was no ground rescue force available, and they certainly knew there was no going back to their helicopter. They may have suspected that things would turn out as they did; nonetheless, they did what they believed to be the right thing. They acted based on Army values, which they had clearly made their own: *loyalty* to their fellow soldiers; the *duty* to stand by them, regardless of the circumstances; the *personal courage* to act, even in the face of great danger; *selfless service,* the willingness to give their all. MSG Gary I. Gordon and SFC Randall D. Shughart lived Army values to the end; they were posthumously awarded Medals of Honor.[1]

"I try to lead by example, by being what I want privates to be. And I expect as much out of them." So says Sergeant Jill Henderson, the first woman to win the Army's Drill Sergeant of the Year award. She can do push-ups with the best of them—thirty-five per minute—and she routinely works seventeen-hour days. Even in the rain and muck, she insists on wearing a crisply pressed uniform and spit-shined boots. Her values are clear, and she lives them. "I lead from the heart. The more I take care of people, the more they take care of me." She tells her trainees in boot camp, "A soldier does all the work. If somebody looks down at you, remember inside that you are the one who carries out the mission. If you stay in the Army, you will become a leader."

James Kouzes and Barry Posner,
The Leadership Challenge, p. 83

Many people naively think that leadership is a matter of a set of skills that the leader uses on *other* people: how to influence others, how to inspire others, how to rally others to a cause. But in our experience, and the Army's leadership does not start with focusing on others; it starts with focusing on oneself. John P. Kotter, an award-winning expert on leadership at the Harvard Business School and the author of *Leading Change* and *What Leaders Really Do*, says, "I suspect a lot of people just haven't been taught: always start with yourself. It is a great rule of thumb for so many things. Start with yourself first! And then go out from there. Don't try to teach mathematics until you've learned it yourself."[2]

As we saw in the previous chapter, leadership is a matter of how to be, not how to do it. Only a person who is comfortable in his or her own skin, who has a strong set of values, who behaves consistently with those values, who demonstrates self-discipline, can begin to lead others. Recognizing this truth, the Army's approach to leadership development focuses squarely on personal development and personal values, on *character*.

"Character helps you know what's right and do what's right, all the time and at whatever the cost," *Army Leadership* states. "Character is made up of two interacting parts: values and attributes. Stephen Ambrose, speaking about the Civil War, said that 'at the pivotal point in the war it was always the character of individuals that made the difference.' Army leaders must be those critical individuals of character themselves and in turn develop character in those they lead." Harvard professor and former Army Colonel Scott Snook says, "The real leverage in developing leaders has to do with the *Be* component. Give me a soldier who has that part right, and I can teach her to do anything. Give me a soldier who doesn't, and all the knowledge and skills in the world will not make up for a lack of character."[3] In this chapter, we look at the Army's approach to values and leadership attributes, and then offer some guidelines for translating that approach into civilian life.

Why Values Are Critical

In a democratic society, the values of the armed forces are critical. It is the set of values that those serving in the armed forces possess that determines whether they will use the weapons of war to support or subvert democratic institutions. We have all seen countries around the world where the armed forces have used their power to promote their own interests and those of their commanders over the interests of society through coups, revolutions, or intimidation of elected officials. We are fortunate in America that the values of our armed forces have consistently led to the support of democracy and the rule of law. It is probably no accident that that first Army value is loyalty.

In civilian organizations, values are no less critical. We will return to this issue later in this chapter.

What are values? "Our values are the principles that help guide our behavior," according to Anne Deering, Robert Dilts, and Julian Russel in *Alpha Leadership*. "Our values reflect the core of our identify, and are the lens through which we execute our goals. Values unite a company around its purpose and vision. . . . The congruence of our stated values and our actual practices is pivotal to the organization's success."[4]

The Army values are loyalty, duty, respect, selfless service, honor, integrity, and personal courage (see Exhibit 2.1). Notice that these values are not specifically war-related. They are deeper, more universal values. And most importantly, they accord with values we are taught in our families, our schools, our churches, synagogues, and mosques. Only in this way can they be deeply felt, made congruent, as Deering says.

Army values are more than a system of rules. They're not just a code tucked away in a drawer or a list in a dusty book. These values tell soldiers what they need to be, every day, in every action they take. Army values form the very identity of the Army, the solid rock upon which everything else stands, especially in combat. Army

Exhibit 2.1. Army Values

Loyalty: **Bear true faith and allegiance to the U.S. Constitution, the Army, your unit, and other soldiers.**

Since before the founding of the Republic, the Army has respected its subordination to its civilian political leaders. This subordination is fundamental to preserving the liberty of all Americans. Soldiers begin their Army career by swearing allegiance to the Constitution, the basis of our government and laws. Beyond their allegiance to the Constitution, soldiers have an obligation to be faithful to the Army—the institution and its people—and to their unit or organization.

Loyalty is a two-way street: leaders should not expect loyalty without being prepared to give it as well. Leaders can neither demand loyalty nor win it from their people by talking about it. The loyalty of your people is a gift they give you when, and only when, you deserve it—when you train them well, treat them fairly, and live by the concepts you talk about. Leaders who are loyal to their subordinates never let them be misused.

Duty: **Fulfill your obligations.**

Duty begins with everything required by law, regulation, and orders, but it includes much more than that. Army leaders take the initiative, figuring out what needs to be done before being told what to do. Professionals do their work not just to the minimum standard but to the very best of their ability. Soldiers commit to excellence in all aspects of their professional responsibility so that when the job is done they can look back and say, "I couldn't have given any more."

In extremely rare cases, a soldier may receive an illegal order. Duty requires the soldier to refuse to obey it. Soldiers have no choice but to do what's ethically and legally correct.

Respect: **Treat people as they should be treated.**

Respect for the individual forms the basis for the rule of law, the very essence of what makes America. In the Army, respect means recognizing and appreciating the inherent dignity and worth of all people. As America becomes more culturally diverse, Army leaders must be aware that they will deal with people from a wider range of ethnic, racial, and religious backgrounds. Effective leaders are tolerant of beliefs different from their own as long as those beliefs don't conflict with Army values, are not illegal, and are not unethical. One shows respect by seeking to understand other people's background, see things from their perspective, and appreciate what's important to them. An Army leader must also foster a climate in which everyone is treated with dignity and respect regardless of race, gender, creed, or religious belief.

Respect is also an essential component for the development of disciplined, cohesive, and effective warfighting teams. In the deadly confusion of combat, soldiers often overcome incredible odds to accomplish the mission and protect the lives of their comrades. This spirit of selfless service and duty is built on a soldier's

Exhibit 2.1. Army Values, Cont'd

personal trust and regard for fellow soldiers. A leader's willingness to tolerate discrimination or harassment on any basis, or a failure to cultivate a climate of respect, eats away at this trust and erodes unit cohesion.

Selfless service: **Put the welfare of the nation, the Army, and subordinates before your own.**
Members of the Army serve the United States. Selfless service means doing what's right for the nation, the Army, the organization, and one's people—and putting these responsibilities above one's own interests. This doesn't mean that soldiers should neglect their families or themselves; in fact, such neglect weakens a leader and can cause the Army more harm than good. Selfless service doesn't mean that a soldier can't have a strong ego, high self-esteem, or even healthy ambition. Rather, selfless service means not making decisions or taking actions that help one's image or one's career but hurts others or sabotages the mission. The Army can't function except as a team, and for a team to work, the individual has to give up self-interest for the good of the whole.

Team members give of themselves so that the team may succeed. In combat some soldiers give themselves completely so that their comrades can live and the mission can be accomplished. But the need for selflessness isn't limited to combat situations. Requirements for individuals to place their own needs below those of their organization can occur during peacetime as well. And the requirement for selflessness doesn't decrease with one's rank, it increases.

Honor: **Live up to all the Army values.**
Honor provides the "moral compass" for character and personal conduct in the Army. Though many people struggle to define the term, most recognize instinctively those with a keen sense of right and wrong, those who live such that their words and deeds are above reproach. The expression "honorable person," therefore, refers to both the character traits an individual actually possesses and the fact that the community recognizes and respects them. Military ceremonies recognizing individual and unit achievement demonstrate and reinforce the importance the Army places on honor.

For an Army leader, honor means putting Army values above self-interest, above career and comfort. For all soldiers, it means putting Army values above self-preservation as well. This honor is essential for creating a bond of trust among members of the Army and between the Army and the nation it serves. The military's highest award is the Medal of Honor. Its recipients didn't do just what was required of them; they went beyond the expected, above and beyond the call of duty. Some gave their own lives so that others could live. It's fitting that the word we use to describe their achievements is "honor."

Exhibit 2.1. Army Values, Cont'd

Integrity: **Do what's right—legally and morally.**

People of integrity consistently act according to principles—not just what might work at the moment. Leaders of integrity make their principles known and consistently act in accordance with them. The Army requires leaders of integrity who possess high moral standards and are honest in word and deed. Being honest means being truthful and upright all the time, despite pressures to do otherwise. Having integrity means being both morally complete and true to yourself.

Leaders can't hide what they do: Army leaders say what they mean and do what they say. People of integrity do the right thing not because it's convenient or because they have no choice. They choose the right thing because their character permits no less.

Personal courage: **Face fear, danger, or adversity (physical or moral).**

Personal courage isn't the absence of fear; rather, it's the ability to put fear aside and do what's necessary. It takes two forms, physical and moral. Good leaders demonstrate both. Physical courage means overcoming fears of bodily harm and doing your duty. It's the bravery that allows a soldier to take risks in combat in spite of the fear of wounds or death. Physical courage is what gets the soldier at Airborne School out the aircraft door. It's what allows an infantryman to assault a bunker to save his buddies.

Moral courage is the willingness to stand firm on values, principles, and convictions—even when threatened. It enables leaders to stand up for what they believe is right, regardless of the consequences. Leaders who take responsibility for their decisions and actions, even when things go wrong, display moral courage. Courageous leaders are willing to look critically inside themselves, consider new ideas, and change what needs changing.

In combat, physical and moral courage may blend together. The right thing to do may not only be unpopular but dangerous as well. Such situations reveal who is a leader of character and who is not.

---

values are nonnegotiable: they apply to everyone and in every situation throughout the Army. They are the power that binds together the members of a noble profession. As a result, the whole is much greater than the sum of its parts. Army values remind Army members and tell the rest of the world—the civilian government, the nation, even enemies—what the Army stands for.

A great civilization is a drama lived in the minds
of a people. It is a shared vision; it is shared norms,
expectations, and purposes. When one thinks of the
world's great civilizations the most vivid images that
crowd in on us are apt to be of the physical monu-
ments left behind—the pyramids, the Parthenon,
the Mayan temples. But in truth, all the physical
splendor was the merest by-product. The civilizations
themselves, from beginning to end, existed in the
minds of men and women. . . .

If we look at ordinary human communities, we
see the same reality: a community lives in the minds
of its members—in shared assumptions, beliefs, cus-
toms, ideas that give meaning, ideas that motivate.
And among the ideas are norms or values. . . .

Every healthy society celebrates its values.
They are expressed in art, in song, in ritual. They
are stated explicitly in historical documents, in cere-
monial speeches, in textbooks. They are reflected in
stories told around the campfire, in the legends kept
alive by old folks, in the fables told to children.
                    John W. Gardner, On Leadership, pp. 13–14

Paul J. Kern, Commanding General of the U.S. Army Materiel Command, who served three combat tours, says, "The values that the Army has established are far-reaching. I've had that reinforced by external, nonmilitary organizations that have told us that the difference between an American soldier and most of the rest of the world is the values they carry with them. They don't come in as occupation forces. They fight like hell and they're the toughest people on the battlefield, then they turn around and apply what we have learned in our own democratic society, establishing those values wherever they happen to be, and then they leave. Values count, they're not just words. People in the culture will be driven by the values expressed by what people do, not by what they say."[5]

Robert Eckert, who served as president of Kraft Foods before being named Mattel's chief executive officer, says, "When I talk to young MBAs and college students, I never ask about jobs on their résumés. I try to understand their values, what is most important to them and whether they will fit here."[6]

In businesses, too often the values that are preached don't really matter to people. The idea that people get up in the morning to pursue shareholder value or exceed customer expectations is silly. "Our personal identity and purpose cannot reside in this type of objective," Anne Deering says. "We need to dig deeper to find what truly drives us—our calling in life—and then to translate this calling back into our work context. And if we find it impossible to make the two worlds congruent, then a fundamental change is essential."

Leadership Attributes

Values form an important part of a leader's character; individuals who aspire to leadership must also possess key personal characteristics, or attributes. People are born with some attributes; for instance, a person's genetic code determines eye, hair, and skin color. However, other attributes—including leader attributes—are learned and can be changed. The Army characterizes leadership attributes as mental, physical, and emotional. The Army expects its leaders to work to improve themselves across all three dimensions.

Mental Attributes

What the Army calls mental attributes don't just include things like intelligence but also characteristics that might be called, and quite rightly, moral. The mental attributes the Army focuses on are will, self-discipline, initiative, judgment, self-confidence, intelligence, and cultural awareness.

Will

Will is the inner drive that compels soldiers and leaders to keep going when they are exhausted, hungry, afraid, cold, and wet—when they can't see their way forward and it seems easier to quit. Will enables soldiers to press the fight to its conclusion. For civilians, will enables leaders to pursue goals, rally the team after setbacks, keep their eye on what matters. Everyone needs that inner drive to accomplish critical tasks.

It's easy to talk about will when things go well. The test of a leader's will comes when things go badly—when events seem to be out of control, when you think your bosses have forgotten you, when the plan doesn't seem to work and it looks like you're going to lose. It's then that you must draw on your inner reserves to persevere—to do your job until there's nothing left to do it with and then to remain faithful to your people, your organization, and your country.

John Gardner talks about this kind of will as a form of courage: "A leader needs. . . courage over time, not just willingness to risk, but to risk again and again, to function well under prolonged stress, to survive defeat and keep going."[7] According to Gardner, true leaders never give up.

Self-Discipline

Self-disciplined people are masters of their impulses. This mastery comes from the habit of doing the right thing. Self-discipline allows Army leaders to do the right thing regardless of the consequences for them or their subordinates. Under the extreme stress of combat, soldiers get cut off, fearing for their lives, and have to act without guidance or knowledge of what's going on around them. In such situations, the leader must maintain discipline in the team, which requires self-discipline first of all.

For leaders in civilian organizations, self-discipline means keeping cool in tense meetings, answering the emotional outbursts of others calmly so that they can regain control, keeping focused on their unit's objectives, and having the courage to change their own behavior when they are asking others to change theirs. Self-discipline means most of all that leaders manage their own emotions. "Emotions are contagious," according to Daniel Goleman, whose book, *Emotional Intelligence*, sparked an explosion of interest and research on how emotions affect performance. "We've all seen it: if someone comes into a meeting upset or angry, and that emotion is not dealt with, it can quickly spread to everyone in the group. More positively, a person with a good sense of humor can quickly get a whole roomful of people laughing."[8] Leaders who cannot manage themselves—who lack self-discipline—will fail at managing others.

Initiative

Leaders are self-starters—they act when there are no clear instructions, adapt when the situation changes or when the plan falls apart. Initiative drives the Army leader to seek a better method, anticipate what must be done, and perform without waiting for instructions. Balanced with good judgment, it becomes *disciplined* initiative, an essential leader attribute. An Army leader doesn't just give orders but also makes clear the intent of those orders, the final goal of the mission. In combat, it's critically important for subordinates to understand their commander's intent. When they are cut off or enemy actions derail the original plan, well-trained soldiers who understand the commander's intent will apply disciplined initiative to accomplish the mission.

"Leaders seize the initiative with enthusiasm, determination, and a desire to make something happen," say Kouzes and Posner. "They embrace the challenge presented by the shifts in their industries or the new demands of the marketplace. They commit themselves to creating exciting new possibilities that make a meaningful difference." Leaders have an eagerness to accept responsibility, "to bear the burden of making the decision, to step forward when no one else will," John Gardner says. Effective leaders do not just have initiative themselves, they also develop it in their subordinates by giving them freedom to maneuver, supporting their ideas, and tolerating honest mistakes.

Judgment

"I learned that good judgment comes from experience and that experience grows out of mistakes," General Omar Bradley once said. Good judgment is the ability to size up a situation quickly, determine what's important, and decide what needs to be done. Seasoned leaders consider a range of alternatives before they act, paying careful attention to the likely consequences of alternative courses. Leaders must often juggle hard facts, questionable data, and gut-level intuition to arrive at a decision. Good judgment means making the best decision for the situation. In the Army, it's a key attribute of the art of command.

In our experience, good judgment comes from certain habits of mind. Those with good judgment are always curious, always learning. They make it their business to know as much about the world as possible, and don't confine their curiosity to their own narrow range of expertise, whatever it may be. They are students of human nature. They listen more than they talk. Because they have a lifetime of inquiry and learning, when a crisis erupts, they have a storehouse of knowledge to rely on beyond their own experience. And because they have developed a habit of listening, they can accept advice. Of course, self-discipline is a cornerstone of good judgment: when emotions are out of control, judgment flees.

Self-Confidence

The Army defines it this way: "Self-confidence is the faith that you'll act correctly and properly in any situation, even one in which you're under stress and don't have all the information you want." Self-confidence is important for leaders and teams. People want self-confident leaders, leaders who understand the situation, know what needs to be done, and demonstrate that understanding and knowledge. Self-confident leaders instill self-confidence in their people. In combat, self-confidence helps soldiers control doubt and reduce anxiety. Together with will and self-discipline, self-confidence helps leaders act—do what must be done in circumstances where it would be easier to do nothing—and convince their people to act as well. Self-confidence does not mean arrogance, a certainty of knowledge. In fact, people who are self-confident display that confidence when they are willing to listen openly to others.

Self-confidence comes from competence; it's based on mastering skills, which takes hard work and dedication. It also comes from seeking out a wide variety of challenges that test abilities and provide learning opportunities. It comes from learning to deal with mistakes and setbacks and picking oneself up again afterward. Self-confidence must be earned; it cannot be bestowed by rank or promotions or come as a gift from others.

Intelligence

Intelligence is not simply brainpower. We have all known brilliant people who couldn't find their way home after dark. Napoleon observed how careful attention and hard work mattered more than sheer brilliance: "It is not genius which reveals to me suddenly and secretly what I should do in circumstances unexpected by others; it is thought and meditation."

Although some people are smarter than others, the Army calls on everyone to develop the capabilities they have. Leaders use their intelligence to learn and reflect; then they apply what they learn. Intelligence starts with the realization that one doesn't have all the answers and a willingness to learn. When things don't go quite the way they intended, intelligent leaders are confident enough to step back and ask, "Why did things turn out that way?" Then they are smart enough to build on their strengths and avoid making the same mistake again. The After Action Review is standard practice in the Army, and a major source of learning. We discuss After Action Reviews in Chapter Seven.

Cultural Awareness

Culture is a group's shared set of beliefs, values, and assumptions about what's important as practiced by the group or organization. Since the Army is at least as diverse as American society, and operates in far-flung locations across the globe, Army leaders need to be aware of cultural factors in three contexts: they must be sensitive to the different backgrounds of their people; they must be aware of the culture of the country in which their organization is operating; and they must take into account their partners' customs and traditions when working with forces of another nation.

Both in the Army and in all organizations across America, people come from widely different backgrounds. They are shaped by their schooling, race, gender, and religion as well as a host of other influences. Successful leaders not only recognize that people are different but value them because of their differences, because they are people. The leader's job in the Army—or in any organization—isn't to make everyone the same, but to take advantage of the fact that everyone is different and build a cohesive team with an appreciation of differences.

The Army teaches that it is impossible to predict how the talents of an individual or group will contribute to mission accomplishment. For example, during World War II, U.S. Marines from the Navajo nation formed a group of radio communications specialists dubbed the Navajo Code Talkers. The code talkers used their native language—a unique talent—to handle command radio traffic, which thwarted even the best Japanese code breakers. Leaders everywhere need to be open to exploring the unexpected contributions that people from diverse backgrounds can make. This requires creating a positive organizational climate that makes best use of the various capabilities of people. This kind of work takes tact, patience, appreciation, and trust.

Physical Attributes

People seldom think of physical fitness as an attribute of good leaders. And if you work in a private company, perhaps you will think this section on health and physical fitness is not relevant to those who have office jobs and never pick up anything heavier than a memo. Yet as John Gardner has pointed out, "Top leaders have stamina and great reserves of vitality. Even the leader of a neighborhood organization is apt to stand far above the average in sheer energy—energy to convene meetings after a hard day's work, to chair long and heated debates, to represent groups before the city council, and so on."[9] Consultant Russ Linden has observed that successful leaders have boundless energy. Stamina and energy come from health and physical fitness.

Health means more than just the absence of illness or injury. It means being sound in both mind and body. It is a positive state of well-being. The Army takes a keen interest in the health of its soldiers for a very simple reason: healthy soldiers can perform under extremes in temperature, humidity, and other conditions better than unhealthy ones. Moreover, a soldier unable to fight because of dysentery or other disease is as much a loss as one who's wounded. In the Army, leaders take care of themselves and encourage others to do so as well by undergoing routine physical exams, practicing good hygiene, and avoiding things that degrade health, such as substance abuse, obesity, and smoking.

Physical fitness goes beyond simply staying healthy. Physical fitness is the ability to function effectively in physical work, training, and other activities and still have enough energy left over to handle any emergencies that may arise. The Army's standards of physical fitness include cardiorespiratory endurance, strength, flexibility, and other matters.

Although physical fitness is a crucial element of success in battle, it is also critical in any stressful situation or when intense concentration is required. Wherever they are, people who are physically fit feel more competent and confident. That attitude reassures and inspires those around them. Physically fit leaders in and out of the military can handle stress better, work longer and harder, and recover faster than ones who are not fit.

A leader who promotes the physical, mental, emotional, and spiritual health of employees is investing in success. Our health and physical fitness is influenced by the organizations we work in, and in turn we influence the health of the organization—what goes around comes around.

Beyond maintaining their health and physical fitness, Army leaders are expected to look like soldiers, to know how to wear the uniform and wear it with pride, to carry themselves well and exhibit military courtesy and appearance. Skillful use of one's professional bearing—fitness, courtesy, and military appearance—helps Army leaders manage difficult situations.

Many companies in the private sector have learned this lesson as well. Dress codes require suits and good grooming. This isn't just a matter of looking good for customers, but of showing respect for one's colleagues at work. In and out of the military, it is important for leaders to look like leaders, treat everyone with courtesy and respect, and maintain self-control.

Emotional Attributes

As leaders, our emotional attributes—self-control, balance, and stability—contribute to how we feel and how we interact with others. In and out of the military, people are human beings with hopes, fears, concerns, and dreams. Army leaders who understand that will and endurance come from emotional energy possess a powerful leadership tool. Leaders who help team members tap into their emotional energy enable their team to accomplish amazing feats in tough times. What distinguishes a true leader from a manager is the ability to mobilize the energy of others to execute the strategy. Noel Tichy in *The Leadership Engine* said it well: "Being a winning leader means tapping a deep reservoir of emotional energy. . . . Simply put, a leader's job is to energize others. Notice I don't say it's part of their job; it is their job. . . . Every interaction leaders have is either going to positively energize those around them or negatively energize them."[10]

Leaders who are emotionally mature also have a better awareness of their own strengths and weaknesses. Mature leaders spend their energy on self-improvement; immature leaders spend their energy denying there's anything wrong. Mature, less defensive leaders benefit from constructive criticism in ways that immature people cannot.

Self-control is critical because no one trusts or wants to follow an out-of-control leader whose behavior is erratic and unpredictable. Maintaining self-control inspires calm confidence in subordinates, the coolness under fire so essential to a successful unit. It also encourages feedback from team members, which can expand the leader's sense of what's really going on.

Self-control does not mean keeping emotions bottled up inside, hidden. Emotionally balanced leaders display the right emotion for the situation and can also read others' emotional state. Effective leaders display genuine emotion and passion in ways that help them tap into others' emotions. They draw on their experience and provide their subordinates the proper perspective on events. They have a range of attitudes—from relaxed to intense—with which to approach situations and can choose the one appropriate to the circumstances. Such leaders know when it's time to send a message that things are urgent and how to do that without throwing the organization into chaos. They also know how to encourage people at the toughest moments and keep them driving on.

Effective leaders are stable, levelheaded under pressure and fatigue, and calm in the face of danger. These characteristics calm their subordinates, who are always looking to their leader's example. True leaders display the emotions they want their people to display; they don't give in to the temptation to do what feels good for them. If you're under great stress, it might feel better to vent—scream, throw things, kick furniture—but that will not help the organization. If you want your subordinates to be calm and rational under pressure, you must be also.

Lessons for Civilian Organizations

If anything should be clear about the Army's approach to developing leaders, it is that it sees the leader as a whole person. The Army realizes that a leader is not just a role—a position in the organizational chart, a cog in the machine—but a person with mental, emotional, and physical dimensions. And people who are serious about leading realize first and foremost that it is their responsibility to develop themselves before they seek to lead others.

The business world could benefit greatly from this whole-person approach. Take a typical 360-degree feedback instrument and its dimensions under leadership. One such instrument includes six dimensions: assertiveness, promoting change, motivating, assigning work, coaching, and empowering. All these dimensions focus on the leader's relationships with others, what a leader does, rather than what a leader is. Although there is nothing wrong with looking at this aspect of leadership, it certainly leaves out the largest dimension, which the Army emphasizes—that is, the leader's own character and how the leader develops himself or herself.

Character helps leaders determine what's right and provides the motivation to do it, whether or not it is easy or convenient. Leaders of character do not take the easy way out. And they set the example for everyone around them. In a person of character, words and deeds blend together seamlessly. The complaint heard today in many organizations—"He talks the talk, but he doesn't walk the walk"—is really a comment on the leader's lack of character. And it often results from focusing on leadership as a set of skills rather than a set of personal values and characteristics.

In their study of effective leadership practices, James Kouzes and Barry Posner discovered that exemplary leaders "model the way." Effective leaders "know that if they want to gain commitment and achieve the highest standards, they must be models of the behavior they expect of others."[11] They must align actions and values, as character demands. Mort Meyerson, former Perot Systems CEO, says, "There are certain durable principles that underlie an organization. The leader should embody those values. They're fundamental. But they have nothing to do with business strategy, tactics, or market share. They have to do with human relationships and the obligation of the organization to its individual members and its customers."[12]

Dean Spitzer, a senior consultant with IBM Business Consulting Services and an experienced leadership coach, says, "Unfortunately, many organizations develop visions and values and then promptly ignore them, or just use them for punitive purposes. Too many leaders give lip service to vision and values at well-programmed retreats, and then put these lofty statements on the shelf when the pressures of daily operations kick in. Leaders should be very careful what they commit to, and they need to appreciate how easy it is for well-intentioned statements to be seen as rank hypocrisy."[13]

Positional leaders who lack character and values are hardly leaders at all in the real sense, even though they may hold the title of president or CEO. As we have seen recently at Enron, Worldcom, Tyco, and Arthur Andersen, the lack of character and values can destroy. When values founder, the world turns upside down. Stockholders are no longer considered owners in whose trust the company acts, but patsies to be fleeced. Likewise, employees are simply sources of money to help prop up stock prices, or scapegoats to be set up when things go wrong. Laws are no longer the expression of the people's sovereignty, but things to find loopholes in. When values are missing or when twisted values become rampant, the organization becomes a corrupt enterprise and often, like the Soviet Union, like Enron, it implodes from within.

Corporate values, organizational values must embrace universal values. In businesses, too often the values that are preached don't really matter to people. As we said earlier, people do not get up in the morning to pursue shareholder value or meet financial projections. Ray Gilmartin, chairman and CEO of Merck & Co., Inc., America's largest drug maker, understands this well. "I was asked in an interview, 'Do you consider your shareholder your most important constituent? Is your primary responsibility to your shareholder?' Guided by the values of the company, I responded that our most important responsibility is to the patient, and that if we fulfill that responsibility our shareholders will benefit." Gilmartin says that companies "must make clear the linkage between values and leadership."[14] Merck's employees take great pride in working for a company providing life-saving medicines to people.

Herb Kelleher, the founder of the phenomenally successful Southwest Airlines, stresses that values must be genuine. "My best lesson in leadership came during my early days as a trial lawyer. Wanting to learn from the best, I went to see two of the most renowned litigators in San Antonio try cases. One sat there and never objected to anything, but was very gentle with witnesses and established a rapport with the jury. The other was an aggressive, thundering hell-raiser. And both seemed to win every case." That's when he learned that it is useless to look for the one right path. "People with different personalities, different approaches, different values succeed not because one set of values or practices is superior, but because their values and practices are *genuine*. And when you and your organization are true to yourselves—when you deliver results *and* a singular experience—customers can spot it from thirty thousand feet."[15]

The Army says that its values show soldiers and the world at large "who we are and what we stand for." Do your values and those of your organization show those inside and outside your organization who you are and what you stand for? Does your organization focus on whole people, their values, and their mental, emotional, and physical well-being? Can everyone spot what you stand for from thirty thousand feet?

"Big Red One"
Armored to Teeth with Smiles in Kirkuk

By Pfc. Brandon R. Aird, 173rd Airborne Brigade
Public Affairs Office, Vicenza, Italy

KIRKUK, Iraq (*Army News Service, April 23, 2003*)—*Soldiers of the 1st Infantry Division's 3rd Brigade are conducting armored patrols through the*

streets of this northern Iraq city to prevent crime,
ethnic harassment, and gather information on local
military groups.

During a patrol in downtown Kirkuk Saturday,
barefoot children chased Bradley Fighting Vehicles
and M113 Armored Personnel Carriers, asking
soldiers questions.

"We had one kid chase us for a few miles,"
said Sgt. Jeffrey L. Reed, Bravo Company, 2/2nd
Infantry, 1st Inf. Div. "Every time we thought
we lost him he would show up again," he added,
laughing.

One teenager ran up to the patrol to give soldiers
mortar rounds he had found.

"The kid gave us seven mortar rounds," said
Reed. "It's nice to be getting these off the streets, but
there's much more out there. A few days ago we
found seven trucks full of rocket-propelled grenades,
hand grenades, and other ammunition."

Looking for weapons and ordnance is a major
focus of the patrols, along with identifying flags above
military compounds in the area.

"By identifying flags we can tell who we're
dealing with," said 2nd Lt. Jeffrey M. Bartel, a platoon leader with HHC, 2/63rd Armor. "So far we've
noticed our area of operation has a high number of
Turkish and Kurdish residents. It's important for us to
identify ethnic backgrounds so we can try to prevent
ethnic harassment."

After the sun went down, soldiers dismounted
from their vehicles (except drivers and vehicle commanders) and walked on foot, talking to the locals.
Soldiers talked to residents about a wide variety of
things.

"I was asking residents how they felt about us being here," said Bartel. "Most of the people were delighted that we're here. Only one person told me he didn't want us here, but he still invited me back to his house for food."

"Most of the questions I was asking was just normal stuff," said Reed. "How old you are? What's your name? Do you like us being here?"

The patrol ended with soldiers getting back in their vehicles and driving off with whistles and applause from residents showing their appreciation.

"It's an awesome feeling," said Reed. "To be making a difference and actually seeing it in people's faces."

[http://www4.army.mil/ocpa/read.php?story_id_key=90]

PEOPLE ARE AT THE CORE

The Army Is People

In September 1944 on the Cotentin Peninsula in France, the commander of a German stronghold under siege by an American force sent word that he wanted to discuss surrender terms. German Major General Hermann Ramcke was in his bunker when his staff escorted the assistant division commander of the U.S. 8th Infantry Division down the concrete stairway to the underground headquarters. Ramcke addressed Brigadier General Charles D. W. Canham through an interpreter: "I am to surrender to you. Let me see your credentials." Pointing to the dirty, tired, disheveled—but victorious—American infantrymen who had accompanied him and were now crowding the dugout entrance, the American officer replied, "These are my credentials."

The measure of leadership is not the quality of the head, but the tone of the body. The signs of outstanding leadership appear primarily among the followers. Are the followers reaching their potential? Are they learning? Serving? Do they achieve the required results? Do they change with grace? Manage conflict?[1]

In the previous chapter, we looked at how the Army focuses squarely on developing leaders as whole people. As we noted, the basis of leadership—the foundation effective leaders build on—is inside the person of the leader, in his or her values and qualities. Without the appropriate values and qualities, no amount of skill, technique, or rhetoric will do the job—and when the chips are down, when leadership matters most, the would-be leader will falter. But once the foundation is laid in the qualities and character of the leader, skill does matter. Leadership in action is emphatically about using skillful interpersonal relations to pull people together in pursuit of common goals. It's about building teams and creating an environment that maximizes performance in achieving results.

Army leadership doctrine stresses that the Army cannot function except as a team. This team identity doesn't come about just because people take an oath when they join the Army. Rather, the team identity comes out of mutual respect among its members and trust between leaders and subordinates. That bond of trust between leaders and subordinates likewise springs from mutual respect. In this chapter, we look at the Army's approach to the human dimension of leadership. We first examine how Army leaders are expected to lead people as individuals, and then on the group level how they create the right environment in their unit.

Leaders Lead People

As we discussed in Chapter Two, the Army's approach to developing leaders focuses on the leader as a whole person. The Army realizes that a leader is not just a role, a position in the organizational chart, a cog in the machine, but a person with mental, emotional, and physical dimensions. This principle extends to how the Army expects its leaders to lead the people on their teams: as whole people. Regardless of the level, leaders lead people. In the words of former Army Chief of Staff Creighton W. Abrams, "The Army is not made up of people; the Army is people . . . living, breathing, serving human beings. They have needs and interests and desires. They have spirit and will, strengths and abilities. They have weaknesses and faults, and they have means. They are the heart of our preparedness . . . and this preparedness—as a nation and as an Army—depends upon the spirit of our soldiers. It is the spirit that gives the Army . . . life."[2]

In today's world of tight deadlines, narrow specialization, high technology, and conflicting demands, it is all too easy to treat people in an organization as if they were little more than job descriptions, as tools. It is all too easy to forget that the IT guy, the marketing whiz, or the engineer are people first, not just functions and tasks. But treating people as replaceable cogs in a wheel does not build loyalty and commitment. It does not inspire people to put the good of the organization first and foremost. Because, as we have seen, the Army stresses the values of loyalty, duty, and selfless service, among others, it does not make this mistake. It realizes that soldiers at all levels are people, and leaders must engage—and lead—the whole person.

Here is what *Army Leadership* says about the responsibilities of Army leaders for their people:

> Whenever the talk turns to what leaders do, you'll almost certainly hear someone say, "Take care of your soldiers." And that's good advice. In fact, if you add one more clause, "Accomplish the mission and take care of your soldiers," you have guidance for a career. But "taking care of soldiers" is one of those slippery phrases, like the word "honor," that lots of people talk about but few take the trouble to explain. So what does taking care of soldiers mean?
>
> Taking care of soldiers means creating a disciplined environment where they can learn and grow. It means holding them to high standards, training them to do their jobs so they can function in peace and win in war. You take care of soldiers when you treat them fairly, refuse to cut corners, share their hardships, and set the example. Taking care of soldiers encompasses everything from making sure a soldier has time for an annual dental exam to

visiting off-post housing to make sure it's adequate. It also means providing the family support that assures soldiers their families will be taken care of, whether the soldier is home or deployed. Family support means ensuring there's a support group in place, that even the most junior soldier and most inexperienced family members know where to turn for help when their soldier is deployed.

Taking care of soldiers also means demanding that soldiers do their duty, even at the risk of their lives. It doesn't mean coddling them or making training easy or comfortable. In fact, that kind of training can get soldiers killed. Training must be rigorous and as much like combat as is possible while being safe. Hard training is one way of preparing soldiers for the rigors of combat. Take care of soldiers by giving them the training, equipment, and support they need to keep them alive in combat.

As this excerpt indicates, taking care of soldiers extends so far as to their health and families, because whole people need to be healthy and have families they love and care for.

People Skills

Since leadership is about people, it's not surprising to find interpersonal skills or "people skills," at the top of the list of what an Army leader must have. The core interpersonal skills the Army teaches are communicating, supervising, and mentoring and counseling.

Communicating

Leadership is about getting other people to do what you want them to do. It follows that communicating—transmitting information so that it's clearly understood—is an important skill. After all, if people can't understand you, how will you ever let them know what you want? This is Management 101, but too many leaders neglect to make their own expectations clear. People who report to you probably won't meet your expectations if you haven't made them plain. Although some people who have worked with you for a time have learned to read you and interpret your talk, a new employee won't have that advantage. Jean-François Manzoni and Jean-Louis Barsoux, who have extensively studied how leaders deal with performance problems, have discovered that many "performance problems" are actually the result of the leader's failure to communicate clearly and establish clear expectations.[3] In addition to clearly communicating expectations, it is also important to let team members know about one's management style, priorities, and assumptions.

The Army places major emphasis on communication because it is vital in combat. In the stress, confusion, and turmoil of combat, where emotions run high, clear and effective communication is critical to cohesive teamwork. Moreover, the Army stresses that it is important to communicate not only what but also why. As Herb Kelleher, head of Southwest Airlines, once said, "The important thing is to take the bricklayer and make him understand that he's building a home, not just laying bricks." People need to understand what the immediate objective is, and how it fits into the bigger picture. In combat, subordinates may be out of contact with their leaders. Sometimes the plan falls apart because of something unexpected—weather, terrain, enemy action. Sometimes the leader may be killed or wounded. In those situations, subordinates who know the overall purpose of the mission and the commander's intent have the basic information they need to carry on. And if the leader has established a climate of trust, if the leader has trained the subordinate leaders in how and why decisions are made, one of these subordinates is more likely to step up and take charge. If the leader has failed to communicate the larger objective, the overall plan, and how the immediate task fits, then people will not be able to step in and lead when necessary.

At the strategic level, the Army calls this bigger picture *intent*. Intent is the leader's personal expression of a mission's end state and the key tasks the organization must accomplish to achieve it. By describing their intent, organizational leaders highlight the key tasks that, along with the mission, are the basis for subordinates to exercise initiative when unanticipated opportunities arise or when the original concept of operations no longer applies. Clear and concise, the leader's intent includes a mission's overall purpose and expected results. It provides purpose, motivation, and direction, whether the leader is commanding a division or running a staff directorate. An organizational leader visualizes the sequence of activities that will move the organization from its current state to the desired end state and expresses it as simply and clearly as possible.

After establishing a clear and valid intent, the art of organizational leadership lies in having subordinates take actions on their own to transform that intent into reality. Because organizational leaders are likely to be further away from the point of execution in time and space, they must describe the collective goal rather than list tasks for individual subordinates. With clearly communicated purpose and direction, subordinates can then determine what they must do and why. Within that broad framework, leaders empower subordinates, delegating authority to act: "Here's where we're headed, why we're going there, and how we're going to get there." Purpose and direction align the efforts of subordinates working toward common goals. Without clear communication skills, up and down the line, cohesive teamwork is jeopardized.

Besides providing information and direction, clear communication is critical in persuading others to accept a course of action or point of view. Effective leaders want eager and willing followers, which is achieved more by persuasion than by giving directives or orders. Openness to discussing one's position and a positive attitude toward a dissenting view often diffuse tension and save time and resistance in the long run. Well-developed skills of persuasion and openness to working through controversy in a positive way help leaders overcome resistance and build support. These characteristics are particularly important in dealing with peers and other leaders. By reducing grounds for misunderstanding, persuasion reduces time wasted in overcoming unimportant issues. It also ensures involvement of others, opens communication with them, and places value on their opinions—all team-building actions. By demonstrating these traits, leaders also provide an example that subordinates can use in self-development.

In some circumstances, persuasion may be inappropriate. In combat, Army leaders need to make decisions quickly, modifying the decision-making process to fit the circumstances. But this practice of using the directing leadership styles as opposed to more participatory ones should occur when situations are in doubt, risks are high, and time is short—circumstances that often arise in combat. The Army does not promote exact blueprints for success in every context; indeed, that is why it places such emphasis on leadership and teamwork.

The success or failure of any communication is the responsibility of the leader. If it appears that team members don't understand, good leaders check to make sure they have made themselves clear. In fact, it is never safe to assume people understand; wise leaders always check to make sure they have been heard.

In addition to the reasons already discussed, leaders keep their subordinates informed because doing so demonstrates trust, because sharing information can relieve stress, and because information allows subordinates to determine what they need to do to accomplish the mission when circumstances change. By informing them of a decision—and as clearly as possible, the reasons for it—leaders show others they're important members of the team. Accurate information also relieves unnecessary stress and helps keep rumors under control. (Without an explanation for what's happening, your people will manufacture one—or several—of their own.) Finally, if something should happen to you, the next leader in the chain will be better prepared to take over and accomplish the mission if everyone knows what's going on. Subordinates must understand your intent. In a tactical setting, leaders must understand the intent of their commanders two levels up.

Communicating also goes on from bottom to top. Leaders find out what their people are thinking, saying, and doing by using that most important communication tool: listening. By listening carefully, you can even hear those messages behind what a person is actually saying, the equivalent of reading between the lines. If you take a moment to think about all the training you've received under the heading "communication," you'll see that it probably falls into four broad categories: speaking, reading, writing, and listening. You begin practicing speech early; many children are using words by the age of one. The heavy emphasis on reading and writing begins in school, if not before. Yet how many times have you been taught how to listen? Of the four forms of communication, listening is the one in which most people receive the least amount of formal training. In most leadership situations, communication is a two-way street. So it's equally important as the others. It often comes first because you must listen and understand before you can decide what to say.

The most effective listening is active. Good leaders practice active listening, sending signals to the speaker that say, "I'm paying attention." They nod their heads every once in a while, as if to say, "Yes, I understand." They look the speaker in the eye, giving the speaker their full attention. And they avoid interrupting the speaker, the cardinal sin of active listening.

In face-to-face communication, even in the simplest conversation, there's a great deal going on that has almost nothing to do with the words being used. Nonverbal communication involves all the signals you send with your facial expressions, tone of voice, and body language. Effective leaders know that communication includes both verbal and nonverbal cues.

Be aware of barriers to listening. Don't form your response while the other person is still talking. Don't allow yourself to become distracted by the fact that you're angry, or that you have a problem with the speaker, or that you have lots of other things you need to be thinking about. If you give in to these temptations, you'll miss most of what's being said.

Supervising

Supervising the work of others is a responsibility of Army leaders, especially those on the front line. The Army recognizes that over-centralized authority and oversupervising undermine trust and empowerment. Undersupervising can lead to failure, especially in cases where the leader's intent wasn't fully understood or where people lack the training for the task. In the Army, good leaders know their subordinates and have the skill to supervise at the appropriate level. Training subordinates to act independently is important; that's why direct leaders give instructions on their intent and then allow subordinates to work without constantly looking over their shoulders. Accomplishing the mission is equally important; that's why Army leaders check things—especially conditions critical to the mission (fuel levels), details a soldier might forget (spare batteries for night vision goggles), or tasks at the limit of what a soldier has accomplished before (preparing a new version of a report).

How a leader supervises those on the team can have a big impact on motivation. Motivation grows out of people's confidence in themselves, their unit, and their leaders. Oversupervision can damage that confidence, as can lack of supervision. In the Army, confidence is born in hard, realistic training; it's nurtured by constant reinforcement and through the kind of leadership—consistent, hard, and fair—that promotes trust. Motivation also springs from a person's faith in the larger mission of the organization, a sense of being a part of the big picture.

People want to be recognized for the work they do and they want to be empowered. A leader empowers subordinates by training them to do the job, giving them the necessary resources and authority, getting out of their way, letting them work, and being available to offer guidance.

Part of empowering subordinates is finding out their needs. Army leaders talk to their people: find out what's important to them, what they want to accomplish, what their personal goals are. They give them feedback that lets them know how they're doing. They listen carefully to understand what is meant, not just what is said. They use a subordinate's feedback when it makes sense and let everyone know where the good idea came from. Good leaders realize there's no limit to the amount of good they can do as long as they don't worry about who gets the credit.

Army leaders recognize subordinates in a variety of ways, from a pat on the back to a formal award or decoration. They don't underestimate the power of a few choice words of praise when a person has done a good job. And they don't hesitate to give out awards—commendations, letters, certificates—when appropriate. Napoleon marveled at the motivational power of properly awarded ribbons and medals. He once said that if he had enough ribbon, he could rule the world.

Of course, part of supervising is recognizing when things are not working out. Not everyone is going to deserve recognition. Unlike in many civilian organizations, the Army is very direct about handling poor and inappropriate behavior. In fact, because it is a military organization, it can use forms of punishment unavailable in civilian organizations. But in most, although not all, cases, the Army counsels leaders to try to change the subordinate's behavior by counseling or retraining before resorting to punishment. Here is the advice *Army Leadership* offers on using punishment:

> Using punishment to motivate a person away from an undesirable behavior is effective, but can be tricky. Sound judgment must guide you when administering punishment. Before you punish a subordinate, make sure the subordinate understands the reason for the punishment. With an open mind and without prejudging, listen to the subordinate's side of the story. Since people tend to live up to their leader's expectations, tell them, "I know you

can do better than that. I expect you to do better than that." Consult your leader or supervisor before you punish a subordinate. They'll be aware of policies you need to consider and may be able to assist you in changing the subordinate's behavior. Avoid threatening a subordinate with punishment. Making a threat puts you in the position of having to deliver on that threat. In such a situation you may end up punishing because you said you would rather than because the behavior merits punishment. This undermines your standing as a leader. Let the subordinate know that it's the behavior—not the individual—that is the problem. "You let the team down" works. "You're a loser" sends the wrong message. Never humiliate a subordinate; avoid public reprimand.

Although civilian organizations rarely talk of "punishment," it does happen, and often behind the scenes in indirect ways that are not acknowledged as punishment. These include reassigning people to an undesirable task or location, freezing them out of the information loop, cutting budgets or other resources, humiliating them in meetings, and so on. The Army's approach and clear guidelines on punishment would be an improvement in many organizations.

The Army teaches its leaders to be always on the lookout for opportunities to develop subordinates, even the ones who are being punished. Army leaders realize that their people—even the ones who cause problems—are still the most important resource they have. When a vehicle is broken, you don't throw it out; you fix it. If one of your people is performing poorly, don't just get rid of the person; try to help fix the problem.

Mentoring and Counseling

One of the most important duties of leaders at all levels is to develop subordinates. Mentoring plays a big part in developing competent and confident future leaders. In the Army, mentoring isn't limited to "high-potentials," or a few favorites. Army leaders are taught to provide inclusive, real-life leader development for every subordinate. Because leaders don't know which of their subordinates today will be the most significant contributors and leaders in the future, they strive to provide all their subordinates with the knowledge and skills necessary to become the best they can be—for the Army and for themselves.

Counseling is an interpersonal skill essential to effective mentoring. Effective counseling helps subordinates develop personally and professionally. The Army values of loyalty, duty, and selfless service require Army leaders to counsel their subordinates. The values of honor, integrity, and personal courage require giving team members straightforward feedback. And the Army value of respect requires leaders to find the best way to communicate that feedback so that subordinates understand it. According to *Army Leadership*, "These Army values all point to the requirement for you to become a proficient counselor."

Mentoring begins with the leader setting the right example. An Army leader mentors people every day in a positive or negative way, depending on how he or she lives and acts on Army values. When a leader lives up to Army values, mentoring shows subordinates a mature example of values, attributes, and skills in action. It encourages them to develop their own character and leader attributes accordingly. Mentoring techniques include teaching, developmental counseling, and coaching.

Army leaders use developmental counseling—or coaching—with people on their team to achieve individual or organizational goals. A consistent developmental counseling program—face-to-face—ensures that the people a leader is responsible for know where they stand and what they should be doing to improve their performance and develop themselves. Coaching involves a leader's assessing performance based on observations, helping the subordinate develop an effective plan of action to sustain strengths and overcome weaknesses, and supporting the subordinate and the plan. Army leaders are encouraged to make time on an ongoing basis to discuss performance objectives and provide meaningful assessments and feedback. That way, no evaluation report, whether positive or negative, will be a surprise.

Setting the example is a powerful leadership tool: if you counsel your subordinates, your subordinate leaders will counsel theirs as well. The way you counsel is the way they'll counsel. Your people emulate your behavior. The significance of your position as a role model can't be overstated. It's a powerful teaching tool, for developmental counseling as well as other behaviors.

The Army is already culturally diverse and is becoming increasingly technologically complex. In this environment, some people may seek advice and counseling from informal relationships in addition to their leadership chain. Such relationships can be particularly important for women, minorities, and those in specialties who have relatively few role models nearby.

This situation in no way relieves the leader of any of his or her responsibilities regarding caring for and developing people. Rather, being sensitive to team members' professional development and cultural needs is part of the cultural awareness leader attribute. Army leaders must know their people and take advantage of every resource available to help their subordinates develop as leaders, including other leaders who have skills or attributes different from theirs.

As leaders assume positions of greater responsibility, as the number of people for whom they are responsible increases, they need to do even more to develop their subordinates. More, in this case, means establishing a leadership development program for the leader's unit or organization. It also means encouraging subordinates to take actions to develop themselves personally and professionally.

The Army's emphasis on mentoring is shared by some of the best companies in the private sector. Lauren Cantlon and Bob Gandossy at Hewitt Associates, a management consulting firm, conducted a study of the top companies for developing leaders and found that their top executives often spend 50 to 60 percent of their time mentoring and developing leaders. "Leaders lead—and it's personal. One senior executive we spoke with at IBM mentors over thirty people beyond his own direct reports. He makes a point to spend at least thirty minutes each quarter with each of them. He also initiated a reverse mentoring process, where someone who's been with the company less than two years has the opportunity to coach him. He believes that this provides him the benefit of learning and receiving feedback from a different perspective, and finds this process personally motivating—motivating for the younger coaches as well."[4] Thomas J. Tierney, chairman of the Bridgespan Group, says that at outstanding companies, top leaders allocate time to recruiting, developing, and motivating people. The top leaders are "starmakers," nurturing future generations of leadership and aligning their interests with the organization's goals. For young people, the time of more senior people is the most valuable currency. Knowing that the firm's leaders are personally interested in their success has great meaning for them.

Creating the Right Environment

In addition to communicating with, supervising, and counseling the individuals on their team, leaders also have a powerful role in shaping the environment of the team or unit. Do people speak up with good ideas or keep them to themselves? Is diversity honored at all times and in all ways? Do people cooperate with each other, offer help to each other—or do they just keep their heads down and focus on their own individual tasks? How is conflict handled when disagreements occur? The sum total of all these and many other aspects of behavior create the environment of the group, its climate or culture.

The Army knows that its climate and culture are tremendously important. When military historians discuss great armies, they write about weapons and equipment, training, and the national cause. They may mention sheer numbers (as Voltaire said, "God is always on the side of the heaviest battalions") and all sorts of other things that can be analyzed, measured, and compared. However, some also write about another factor equally important to success in battle, something that can't be measured: the emotional element called morale or esprit de corps. High morale is critical to both military and civilian organizations. "It is the spirit which we bring to the fight that decides the issue. It is morale that wins the victory," General George C. Marshall said.

Morale is a measure of how people feel about themselves, their team, and their leaders. High morale comes from good leadership, shared hardship, and mutual respect. It's an emotional bond that springs from common values like loyalty to fellow soldiers and a belief that the organization will care for families. High morale results in a cohesive team that enthusiastically strives to achieve common goals. Army leaders know that morale, the essential human element, holds the team together and keeps it going in the face of the terrifying and dispiriting things that occur in war. When people are part of a disciplined and cohesive team, they gain proficiency, are motivated, and willingly subordinate themselves to organizational needs. People who sense they're part of a competent, well-trained team act on what the team needs; they're confident in themselves and feel a part of something important and compelling. These team members know that what they do matters and discipline themselves.

An organization's climate and culture are key factors in determining morale. The Army uses *culture* to refer to the environment of the Army as an institution and of major elements or communities within it. *Climate* in the Army refers to the environment of smaller units and organizations.

Climate

Taking care of people and maximizing their performance also depends on the organizational climate a leader creates. An organization's climate is the way its members feel about their organization. Climate comes from people's shared perceptions and attitudes, what they believe about the day-to-day functioning of their outfit. These things have a great impact on their motivation and the trust they feel for their team and their leaders. Climate is changeable: to a large extent it depends on a network of the personalities in a small organization. As people come and go, the climate changes. When a soldier says, "My last platoon sergeant was pretty good, but this new one is great," the soldier is talking about one of the many elements that affect organizational climate.

The members' collective sense of the unit or team—its organizational climate—is directly attributable to the leader's values, skills, and actions. The leader establishes the climate of the organization, no matter how small it is or how large. Army leaders who do the right things for the right reasons, even when it would be easier to take an easy way out, create a healthy organizational climate. In fact, it's the leader's behavior that has the greatest effect on the organizational climate. That behavior signals to every member of the organization what the leader will and will not tolerate. Here are some of the key aspects of an organizational climate that the Army expects leaders to ask about themselves and their units:

Does the leader set clear priorities and goals?

Is there a system of recognition, rewards, and punishments? Does it work?

Do the leaders know what they're doing? Do they admit when they're wrong?

Do leaders seek input from subordinates? Do they act on the feedback they're provided?

In the absence of orders, do junior leaders have authority to make decisions that are consistent with the leader's intent?

Are there high levels of internal stress and negative competition in the organization? If so, what's the leader doing to change that situation?

Do the leaders behave the way they talk? Is that behavior consistent with Army values? Are they good role models?

Do the leaders lead from the front, sharing hardship when things get tough?

Do leaders talk to their organizations on a regular basis? Do they keep their people informed?

Ethics is a critical component of any organization's climate. The Army makes it plain that it expects leaders at all levels to be ethical standard-bearers. Every leader is charged with building an ethical climate in his or her unit that demands and rewards behavior consistent with Army values. Setting a good ethical example doesn't necessarily mean subordinates will follow it. Some of them may feel that circumstances justify unethical behavior. Therefore, a leader must constantly maintain a feel for the organization's current ethical climate and take prompt action to correct any shortcomings. In this regard, a leader needs to be a careful observer and a patient listener.

In the Army, it is especially important for people to have confidence in the organization's ethical environment because much of what is necessary in war goes against the grain of the values individuals bring into the Army. For example, a soldier's conscience may tell him it's wrong to take human life while the mission of the unit calls for exactly that. Without a strong ethical climate that lets that soldier know his duty, the conflict of values may sap the soldier's will to fight.

A climate that promotes Army values and fosters the warrior ethos encourages learning and promotes creative performance. The foundation for a positive organizational climate is a healthy ethical climate, but that alone is insufficient. Characteristics of successful organizational climates include a clear, widely known intent; well-trained and confident soldiers; disciplined, cohesive teams; and trusted, competent leadership.

To create such a climate, organizational leaders recognize mistakes as opportunities to learn, create cohesive teams, and reward leaders of character and competence. Organizational leaders value honest feedback and constantly use all available means to maintain a feel for the environment. Staff members who may be good sources for straightforward feedback include equal opportunity advisers and chaplains. Methods for obtaining feedback may include town hall meetings, surveys, and councils. And of course, personal observation—getting out and talking to civilian employees of the Army, soldiers, and family members—brings organizational leaders face-to-face with the people affected by their decisions and policies. Organizational leaders' consistent, sincere effort to see what's really going on and fix things that are not working right can result in mutual respect throughout their organizations. They must know the intricacies of the job, trust their people, develop trust among them, and support their subordinates.

Organizational leaders who are positive, fair, and honest in their dealings and who are not afraid of constructive criticism encourage an atmosphere of openness and trust. Their people willingly share ideas and take risks to get the job done well because their leaders strive for more than compliance; they seek to develop subordinates with good judgment.

Culture

Culture is a longer-lasting, more complex set of shared expectations than climate. Whereas climate is how people feel about their organization right now, culture consists of the shared attitudes, values, goals, and practices that characterize the larger institution. It's deeply rooted in long-held beliefs and customs. Leaders use the culture to let their people know they're part of something bigger than themselves, that they have responsibilities not only to the people around them but also to those who have gone before and those who will come after. Culture is never completely codified in a formal rulebook or a policy manual, even in the Army. Instead, it is a set of invisible guideposts that define how people should behave. It establishes the do's and the don'ts at all organizational levels. It also helps to tell people inside and outside the organization "who we are."

Some leaders seem to believe that they can legislate behavior, attitudes, and values through edicts and job descriptions. But culture has more influence on behavior than any job description or corporate policy ever written. Although the Army has plenty of policies and procedures, manuals, and job descriptions, it realizes that these cannot dictate behavior in the heat of combat, where quick judgment and fast action are required and where soldiers may be cut off from their leaders. Nor do policies and procedures generate the high morale that the Army needs. Culture is a dominant force in determining how members of the Army behave when the stakes are highest.

Over time, an institution's culture becomes so embedded in its members that they may not even notice how it affects their attitudes. The institutional culture becomes second nature and influences the way people think, the way they act in relation to each other and outside agencies, and the way they approach the mission. Culture shapes Army customs and traditions through doctrine, policies, and regulations, and the philosophy that guides the institution. Professional journals, historical works, ceremonies—even the folklore of the organization—all contain evidence of the Army's institutional culture.

A sense of belonging is vitally important in the Army. Soldiers draw strength from knowing they're part of a tradition. Remember General Marshall's words: "It is morale that wins the victory." Most meaningful traditions have their roots in the institution's culture. Many of the Army's everyday customs and traditions are there to remind today's soldiers that they are the latest addition to a long line of American soldiers. Soldiers are encouraged to think of how their daily life connects them to the past and to American soldiers not yet born: the uniforms and decorations, the martial music that punctuates the day, the way people salute, the stories that are told, and Army values such as selfless service are all reminders of tradition and culture.

One way the Army's institutional culture affirms the importance of individuals is through its commitment to leader development. In essence, this commitment declares that its people are the Army's future. By committing to broad-based leader development, the

Army has redefined what it means to be a soldier. In fact, Army leaders have even changed the appearance of American soldiers and the way they perform. Introducing height and weight standards, raising PT standards, emphasizing training and education, and deglamorizing alcohol have all fundamentally changed the Army's institutional culture.

Lessons for Civilian Organizations

A recent report by the Brookings Institution on intangible assets—things such as patents, copyrights, brands, and employee know-how—shows that they are becoming a larger factor in today's organizations. "Wealth and growth in today's economy are primarily driven by intangible (intellectual) assets. Physical and financial assets are rapidly becoming commodities," according to the report. Brookings estimates that in 1978, the book value of the tangible assets of publicly traded corporations accounted for more than 83 percent of the market value of those companies. Today, that figure has fallen to below 40 percent.

Human capital, the sum total of an organization's knowledge, skills, and abilities, makes up a large portion of many companies' intangible assets. Some large investors believe there is a link between human capital activities and long-term shareholder value, according to a recent Conference Board report. In this climate, all organizations need to make sure all their members have the people skills needed to maximize the talent in the organization. Here are some of the lessons we take away from the Army's approach to teaching interpersonal skills and creating an organizational climate and culture that encourages top performance.

Focus on People, Not Organizational Charts, Incentive Systems, or Policies

Ultimately, it is people who produce results, not job descriptions, functions, or procedures. Though people are hired for a set of skills and experiences, these skills and experiences are always packaged as part of a whole person with hopes and aspirations, physical and spiritual needs, and a web of influences from family, faith, and community. The Army always focuses on the whole person. Does your company?

Take Care of Your People

This may seem anachronistic in today's world, where paternalistic employment practices seem like a relic from the first half of the twentieth century and where people are told to manage their careers as part of a "You, Inc." strategy—to see themselves as independent contractors even as they work their way up the organization chart. Increasingly, the relationship between employers and employees is seen as short-term and contractual. The Army has contractual relationships with its members too, but that does not stop it from placing a premium on their care. Companies that do not want their people to be constantly engaged in calculations of rational self-interest work hard to create a sense of community and belonging, even as they acknowledge that the old promises of lifetime employment are no longer tenable.

Relentlessly Communicate the Big Picture

People need to understand what the immediate objective is, and how it fits into the bigger picture. The Army stresses this because it is the only way to ensure focused action in combat, where leaders may be incapacitated and plans may fall apart. Companies in the private sector who strive to provide superior customer service or exemplary new products also realize that leadership needs to be dispersed to meet these goals, and that the only way to disperse leadership is to communicate the how and why in addition to the what. Southwest Airlines has built a very successful record in a deeply troubled industry by taking this approach. Remember Herb Kelleher's words: "The important thing is to take the bricklayer and make him understand that he's building a home, not just laying bricks."

It is only when everyone in the organization shares the same information and sees the big picture that they can all pull together to achieve extraordinary results. Today's organizations are too big, too complex to be managed from the top down. Says Harvard's leadership expert John Kotter, "Today's organizations need heroes at every level. To truly succeed in a turbulent world, more than half the workforce needs to step up to the plate in some arena and provide change leadership. Most of this leadership will be modest. It might be a young sales rep who makes the company see a critical new opportunity, or a summer intern who helps put together a vivid demonstration of a problem. It is the sum of all these heroic actions—large and small— that enables organizations to change in significant ways."[5]

Mentor and Counsel All Employees

Don't just focus on potential stars on the one hand, or on clear underperformers on the other. Virtually every person in an organization has untapped potential that can be cultivated. As we discussed, the Army's emphasis on mentoring is shared by some of the best companies in the private sector. Lois Zachary, an executive coach and expert on mentoring, says, "In today's competitive business environment, the need for continuous learning has never been greater. At the same time, the hunger for human connection and relationship has never been more palpable. It is no surprise that mentoring has become a basic leadership competency. Leaders who do not learn and do not promote learning within their organizations often end up thwarting their own ability to lead effectively. It is the leader's responsibility to serve as a role model, to mentor the next generation of leaders, and to make sure that continuous opportunities for learning and development are provided. When leaders strengthen themselves, they simultaneously enhance their ability to strengthen others."[6]

Zachary points to John Steinbrunner, chair of Watson Wyatt's Global Contingency Planning Task Force, who mentors younger associates because it gives him an opportunity to stay in touch with their career aspirations and fears, develop the next generation of leaders, and reinforce his own learning.

To repeat a key theme, the Army's focus on mentoring and counseling emphasizes the whole person with emotions, feelings, aspirations, and needs. People in today's organizations have usually been immersed in their education and training with an analytical, number-crunching approach to management. John Kotter says, "All through our lives we have been taught to overrely on what you might call the memo approach—the nineteen logical reasons to change." But logic doesn't inspire people, doesn't motivate them to action. "People change their behavior when they are motivated to do so," Kotter continues, "and that happens when you speak to their feelings. Nineteen logical reasons don't necessarily do it. . . . Imagine, someone once told me, if Martin Luther King had stood up there in front of the Lincoln Memorial and said, 'I have a business strategy.' King didn't do that. He said, 'I have a dream,' and he showed us what his dream was, his picture of the future."[7] In the Army, counseling others helps leaders tap into their emotions—the key to changing behavior. Leaders in civilian organizations who ignore the emotional side of people to focus on facts and analysis are denying themselves a critical tool.

Create a Climate and Culture That Strengthen Morale

Morale not only wins battles, as the Army rightly says, but keeps teams together and productive, wins marketing campaigns, keeps change initiatives on track, helps people handle crises, and brings out the best in people. A climate or culture that saps morale robs the organization of one of its most precious assets. A culture that ensures high morale, on the other hand, promotes employee retention, commitment, and performance. People with high morale provide better service to customers, generate ideas for improvement, handle setbacks, encourage others, and more. With so much at stake, all organizations need to attend to their climate and culture with the same conscious intention as the Army does.

Edgar Schein, perhaps the world's best-known expert on organizational culture and leadership, says that culture can be "created, embedded, developed, and ultimately manipulated, managed, and changed. These dynamic processes of culture creation and management are the essence of leadership." In fact, Schein says, "Leadership and culture are two sides of the same coin." He goes on: "Managers who are trying to change the behavior of subordinates . . . often encounter resistance to change at a level that seems beyond reason."[8] It is beyond reason because it is often emotional and cultural.

How often do you and others in your organization take a step back to assess the kind of climate and culture you are cultivating, whether intentionally or not? Consider the list of questions on leadership and climate shown earlier in this chapter, and ask them of yourself and your organization. Look at your company's orientation program. Does it offer new employees a clear picture of the company's history and traditions? Does it find ways to help employees make a personal connection to those traditions?

LEADING FROM THE FRONT

Get on the Ground

In the late fall of 1950, as United Nations (UN) forces pushed the North Korean People's Army northward, the People's Republic of China prepared to enter the conflict in support of its ally. The UN had air superiority, a marked advantage that had contributed significantly to its tactical and operational successes of the summer and early fall. Nonetheless, daily reconnaissance missions over the rugged North Korean interior failed to detect the movement of nearly a quarter of a million Chinese ground troops across the border and into position in the North Korean mountains.

When the first reports of Chinese soldiers in North Korea arrived at Far East Command Headquarters in Tokyo, intelligence analysts ignored them because they contradicted the information provided by the latest technology—aerial surveillance. Tactical commanders failed to send ground patrols into the mountains. When the Chinese attacked in late November, UN forces were surprised, suffered heavy losses, and were driven from the Chinese border back to the 38th parallel.

When General Matthew B. Ridgway took over the UN forces in Korea in December, he immediately visited the headquarters of every regiment and many of the battalions on the front line. This gave Ridgway a direct, unfiltered look at the situation, and it sent a message to all his commanders: get out on the ground and find out what's going on.

In a broad sense, what leaders do is stage revolutions. They are constantly challenging the status quo and looking around to see if they are doing the right things, or if those things can be done better or smarter. And most importantly, when they do spot something that needs to be changed, they do something about it. In more concrete terms, they do two specific things:

- They see reality—size up the current situation as it really is, not as it *used to be* or as they would *like it to be.*

- They mobilize the appropriate responses.[1]

Army Leadership too tells the story of General Matthew Ridgway. Ridgway's example demonstrates the transformative power of leading from the front. Because his example is so compelling, we think it is worth exploring in some detail. During World War II when Ridgway led the 82nd Airborne Division, far from sitting behind a desk, he jumped with his men in the invasions of Sicily, Italy, and France. His later actions during four months in command of the Eighth Army in Korea bring to life the skills and behavior of those who lead from the front.

At the outbreak of the Korean War in June 1950, General Ridgway was assigned as Army Deputy Chief of Staff, Operations. In December of that year the Eighth Army commander, General Walton Walker, died in a jeep accident, and Ridgway was ordered to take command. At that time, the Eighth Army was defending near the 38th parallel, having completed a three-hundred-mile retreat after the Chinese intervention described in the opening vignette.

The UN defeat left the forces of the Eighth Army in serious disarray. One of its four American divisions, the 2nd, needed extensive replacements and reorganization. Two other divisions, the 25th and 1st Cavalry, were seriously battered. Of the Republic of Korea divisions, only the 1st was in good fighting shape. A British brigade was combat-ready, but it too had suffered substantial losses in helping cover the retreat.

Within twenty-four hours of Walker's death, Ridgway was bound for Korea. During the long flight from Washington, D.C., to General Douglas MacArthur's headquarters in Japan, Ridgway had an opportunity to reflect on what lay ahead. The necessary steps seemed clear: gain an appreciation for the immediate situation from MacArthur's staff, establish his presence as Eighth Army commander by sending a statement of his confidence in them, and then meet with his own staff to establish his priorities. His first message to his new command was straight to the point: "You will have my utmost. I shall expect yours."

During the flight from Japan to his forward command post, Ridgway carefully looked at the terrain upon which he was to fight. The battered Eighth Army had to cover a rugged, hundred-mile-long front that restricted both maneuver and resupply. Poor morale presented a further problem, Ridgway had learned. Many military observers felt that the Eighth Army lacked spirit and possessed little stomach for continuing the bloody battle with the Chinese.

Leading from the front, Ridgway traveled the Army area by jeep for three days, talking with commanders who had faced the enemy beyond the Han River. Ridgway wrote later, "I held to the old-fashioned idea that it helped the spirits of the men to see the Old Man up there, in the snow and the sleet and the mud, sharing the same cold, miserable existence they had to endure." He talked with riflemen and generals from frontline foxholes to corps command posts.

Ridgway was candid, criticizing the spirit of both the commanders and soldiers of the Eighth Army. He was appalled at American infantrymen who didn't patrol, who had no knowledge of the terrain in which they fought, and who failed to know the whereabouts of their enemy. Moreover, the Army was road-bound and failed to occupy commanding terrain overlooking its positions and supply lines. Ridgway also sensed that the Eighth Army—particularly the commanders and their staffs—kept looking over their shoulders for the best route to the rear and planned only for retreat. In short, he found his Army immobilized and demoralized.

Leading from the front loses half its value if it is not visible, and Ridgway believed a commander should publicly show a personal interest in the well-being of his soldiers. He needed to do something to attract notice and display his concern for the frontline fighters. Finding that one of his units was still short of some winter equipment, he dramatically ordered that the equipment be delivered within twenty-four hours. In response, the logistical command made a massive effort to comply, flying equipment from Pusan to the front lines. Everyone noticed. He also ordered—and made sure the order was known—that the troops be served hot meals, with any failures to comply reported directly to him.

As he visited their headquarters, Ridgway spoke to commanders and their staffs. These talks contained many of his ideas about proper combat leadership. He told his commanders to get out of their command posts and up to the front. When commanders reported on terrain, Ridgway demanded that they base their information on personal observation and that it be correct.

Furthermore, he urged commanders to conduct intensive training in night fighting and make full use of their firepower. He also required commanders to personally check that their men had adequate winter clothing, warming tents, and writing materials. In addition, he encouraged commanders to locate wounded who had been evacuated and make every effort to return them to their old units. Finally, the Army commander ordered his officers to stop wasting resources, calling for punishment of those who lost government equipment.

Of course, Ridgway's efforts did not produce immediate miracles. During its first battle under his command in early January 1951, the Eighth Army fell back another seventy miles and lost Seoul, South Korea's capital. The Eighth Army's morale and sense of purpose reached their lowest points ever.

Ridgway began to restore his men's fighting spirit by ordering aggressive patrolling into areas just lost. When patrols found the enemy few in number and not aggressive, the Army commander increased the number and size of patrols. His Army discovered it could drive back the Chinese without suffering overwhelming casualties. Buoyed by these successes, Ridgway ordered a general advance along Korea's west coast, where the terrain was more open and his forces could take advantage of its tanks, artillery, and aircraft. During this advance, General Ridgway also attempted to tell the men of the Eighth Army why they were fighting in Korea. He sought to build a fighting spirit in his men based on unit and soldier pride.

In mid-February of 1951, the Chinese and North Koreans launched yet another offensive in the central area of Korea, where U.S. tanks could not maneuver as readily and artillery could be trapped on narrow roads in mountainous terrain. In heavy fights at Chipyon-ni and Wonju, the Eighth Army, for the first time, repulsed the Communist attacks. The Army's offensive spirit soared as the General quickly followed up with a renewed attack that took Seoul and regained roughly the same positions the Eighth Army had held when he first took command. In late March, barely three months after Ridgway took command, the Eighth Army pushed the Communist forces north of the 38th parallel.

General Ridgway's actions exemplify those expected of Army leaders. He sought to develop subordinate commanders and their staffs by sharing his thoughts and expectations of combat leadership. He felt the pulse of the men on the front, shared their hardships, and demanded they be taken care of. He pushed the logistical systems to provide creature comforts as well as the supplies of war. He eliminated the skepticism of purpose, gave soldiers cause to fight, and helped them gain confidence by winning small victories. Most of all, he led by example, from the front.

Omar N. Bradley, Chairman of the Joint Chiefs of Staff, summed up Ridgway's contributions, "It is not often that a single battlefield commander can make a decisive difference. But in Korea, Ridgway would prove to be that exception. His brilliant, driving, uncompromising leadership would turn the tide of battle like no other general's in our military history."

Leading from the Front at Different Levels

As Ridgway's story makes clear, good Army leaders, even at the highest strategic level, don't sit behind their desks when they send their soldiers out to battle. They get on the ground with them, they lead from the front, and they stay close to the action. They don't make plans in remote isolation, counting on their troops to tough out any situation, without seeing what their soldiers are going through. Army leaders know that graphics on a map symbolize human beings going forward to fight. They get out with their soldiers to see and feel what they're experiencing as well as to influence the battle by their presence. Leaders who stay a safe distance from the front jeopardize operations because they don't know what's going on. They risk destroying their soldiers' trust, not to mention their unit.

Leading from the front presents different challenges at different levels. Leaders at all levels need the same qualities, characteristics, and values. All Army leaders need to *Be, Know, Do*. But leaders at different levels do face different challenges, and meeting those challenges requires different kinds of skills. The Army distinguishes three levels of leadership: direct frontline leadership, organizational leadership, and strategic leadership.

As in any organization, factors that determine an Army position's leadership level can include the position's span of control, its headquarters level, and the extent of the influence the leader holding the position exerts. Other factors include the size of the unit or organization, the type of operations it conducts, the number of people assigned, and its planning horizon. In the Army, a person's rank does *not* always indicate the position's leadership level. A sergeant first class serving as a platoon sergeant works at the direct leadership level. If the same sergeant holds a headquarters job dealing with issues and policy affecting a brigade-size or larger organization, the NCO works at the organizational leadership level. However, most leadership positions are direct leadership positions, and every leader at *every* level acts as a *direct* leader when dealing with immediate subordinates.

Direct Leadership

Direct leadership is face-to-face, first-line leadership. It takes place in those organizations where subordinates are used to seeing their leaders all the time: teams and squads, sections and platoons, companies, batteries, and troops—even squadrons and battalions. The direct leader's span of influence, those whose lives he can reach out and touch, may range from a handful to several hundred people.

Direct leaders develop their subordinates one-on-one; however, they also influence their organization through their subordinates. For instance, a cavalry squadron commander is close enough to his soldiers to have a direct influence on them. They're used to seeing him regularly, even if it is only once a week in garrison; they expect to see him from time to time in the field. Still, during daily operations, the commander guides the organization primarily through his subordinate officers and NCOs.

For direct leaders there is more certainty and less complexity than for organizational and strategic leaders. Direct leaders are close enough to see—very quickly—how things work, how things don't work, and how to address any problems.

Organizational Leadership

Organizational leaders influence several hundred to several thousand people, or more. They do this indirectly, generally through more levels of subordinates than do direct leaders. The additional levels of subordinates can make it more difficult for them to see results. Organizational leaders have staffs to help them lead their people and manage their organization's resources. They establish policies and the organizational climate that support their subordinate leaders.

Organizational leadership skills differ from direct leadership skills in degree, but not in kind. That is, the skill domains are the same, but organizational leaders must deal with more complexity, more people, greater uncertainty, and a greater number of unintended consequences. They find themselves influencing people more through policymaking and systems integration than through face-to-face contact.

Organizational leaders include military leaders at the brigade through corps levels, military and Department of the Army civilian leaders at directorate through installation levels, and civilians at the assistant through undersecretary levels of the Army. They focus on planning, mission, and goal accomplishment over the next two to ten years.

Organizational leaders must make a deliberate effort to lead from the front. Getting out of their offices and visiting the parts of their organizations where the work is done is especially important for organizational leaders. They must make time to get to the field to compare the reports their staff gives them with the actual conditions their people face and the perceptions of the organization and mission they hold. Because of their less-frequent presence among their soldiers and civilians, organizational leaders must use those visits they are able to make to assess how well the commander's intent is understood and to reinforce the organization's priorities.

Strategic Leadership

Strategic leaders include military and Department of the Army civilian leaders at the major command through Department of Defense levels. Strategic leaders are responsible for large organizations and influence several thousand to hundreds of thousands of people. They establish force structure, allocate resources, communicate strategic vision and mission, and prepare their commands and the Army as a whole for their future roles.

Strategic leaders work in an uncertain environment on highly complex problems that affect and are affected by events and organizations outside the Army. Actions of a theater Combatant Commander, for example, may even have an impact on global politics.

(Combatant Commanders run very large, joint organizations that are assigned broad, continuing missions. Theater Combatant Commanders are assigned responsibilities for a geographic area; for example, the Combatant Commander of the U.S. Central Command is responsible for most of southwestern Asia and part of eastern Africa. Functional Combatant Commanders are assigned responsibilities not bounded by geography; for example, the Combatant Commander of the U.S. Transportation Command is responsible for providing integrated land, sea, and air transportation to all services.) Although civilian leaders make national policy, decisions Combatant Commanders make while carrying out that policy may affect whether or not a national objective is achieved. Strategic leaders apply many of the same leadership skills and actions they mastered as direct and organizational leaders; however, strategic leadership requires others that are more complex and indirectly applied.

Strategic leaders concern themselves with the total environment in which the Army functions; their decisions take into account such things as congressional hearings, Army budgetary constraints, new systems acquisition, civilian programs, research, development, and interservice cooperation—just to name a few. Dealing with this complexity means that leading from the front is more complex, too.

The very top leaders in the Army lead from the front in a personal way. As human representatives of the organization, they have a role that cannot be delegated. Army leaders at the strategic level are taught to "vigorously and constantly represent who Army is, what it's doing, and where it's going. The audience is the Army itself as well as the rest of the world. There's an especially powerful responsibility to explain things to the American people, who support their Army with money and lives."

Strategic leaders often do not see their ideas come to fruition on their "watch"; their initiatives may take years to plan, prepare, and execute. On the other hand, some strategic decisions may become a front-page headline in the next morning's newspaper. Strategic leaders have very few opportunities to visit the lowest-level organizations of their commands; thus, their sense of when and where to visit is crucial. Because they exert influence primarily through subordinates, strategic leaders must develop strong skills in choosing and developing good ones.

Lessons for Civilian Organizations

Clearly, leading from the front is critical in the Army. Leading from the front, in our experience, is no less critical in businesses, nonprofits, and government agencies. How many costly and elaborate corporate plans—from restructurings to new product launches—have foundered on the shoals of employee resistance, customer apathy, or poor timing, simply because the leaders who created the plans never got out from behind their desks? How many remote and aloof leaders, when faced with trouble and seeking help, find that "their team" does not support them?

Leading from the front is powerful. Leaders who lead from the front:

- Get critical information about what is happening on the front lines.

- Set the example.

- Provide clear direction to the organization.

- Build morale and the determination to win.

Too often leaders fail to get out in front because they hide behind memos, policies, and procedures. They work indirectly and impersonally to influence others by setting up incentive systems, structures, and policies—and so fail to exercise the power of true leadership. According to Noel Tichy, "Getting the power equation right is tricky in most circumstances. But the toughest place for a leader to do it is with the immediate team. Exercising power face-to-face with close associates is much harder than the impersonal exercise of power through rules, rewards, punishments, guidelines, and the like. Face-to-face encounters require interacting with other emotional beings. The potential for emotional displays makes many leaders uncomfortable. So they avoid it, sometimes by becoming domineering but most often by being too laissez-faire."[2] And, says Tichy, such avoidance often leads to their downfall. As we have already seen, the Army deals with this problem directly, by stressing that people are always whole human beings, not roles, ranks, or positions.

Get Critical Information

Good, useful, reliable information is critical to leadership, yet it is often hard to come by, as the fable of "The Bold Plan" humorously points out (see Exhibit 4.1). John Gardner talked of the importance of getting grassroots experience, frontline experience, "As you go up the line, you're more and more fed with statistics, indices, charts, graphs, symbolic communication. You don't know the soldier in the front line or the salesman behind the counter or the nurse looking after a patient. You don't know what they're experiencing, what

Exhibit 4.1. The Bold Plan

Once upon a time, the Leader came up with a Bold Plan, and sent it forth to all in the organization, asking for constructive feedback.

The frontline workers took a look at it and told their supervisors: "The Bold Plan is a bunch of excrement and it stinks."

And the supervisors went to their department heads and said, "The Bold Plan is a pile of manure and people are holding their noses."

And the department heads went to their divisional managers and said, "The Bold Plan is fertilizer and people are turning up their noses at it."

The divisional managers went to their group vice presidents and said, "It promotes growth and people are nodding their heads."

And the group vice presidents went to the Leader and said, "Your Bold Plan will actively promote strong growth in all our business units; everyone agrees."

And the Leader said, "Implement it."

they're thinking about, what a piece of legislation meant to them."[3] As Ridgway's story clearly demonstrates, leading from the front, getting out on the ground, talking to people, making personal observations, are all critical to getting the sort of information leaders require. The ability to assess a situation accurately and reliably—a critical tool in any leader's arsenal—depends on leading from the front. Only in this way can one get a good feel for the reliability and validity of information and its sources.

Leaders who rely solely on reports and PowerPoint presentations are in danger of blinding themselves to problems in their organization and the opportunities and threats that surround it. There are several different ways to gather information; asking subordinates questions to find out if the word is getting to them, meeting people, and visiting field offices are only a few. Leaders obtain information from various sources so they can compare and make judgments about the accuracy of sources. John Munro, president of Greyhound Bus Lines of Canada, personally visited bus station washrooms unannounced. He not only gained firsthand knowledge of the upkeep of the stations but sent a powerful message to everyone in the organization about the value of cleanliness.

Staff and subordinates manage and process information for a leader, but this doesn't relieve the leader from the responsibility of analyzing information as part of the decision-making process.

Set the Example

As the Army teaches its leaders, "Command is a sacred trust. Those selected to command offer something beyond their formal authority: their personal example and public actions have tremendous moral force. Because of that powerful aspect of their position, people inside and outside the Army see a commander as the human face of 'the system'—the person who embodies the commitment of the Army to operational readiness and care of its people. It's no wonder that organizations take on the personal stamp of their commanders." Whether or not an Army leader holds a command position, however, he or she is expected to set the example.

Setting the example often involves dealing with people face-to-face. As John Gardner observed, "We want to take each other's measure face-to-face. We're more primitive than we think. The memo doesn't do it. We want to hear the tone of voice and see the body language."[4]

Authors Kouzes and Posner, to whom we have referred previously, say, "Exemplary leaders go first. They go first by setting the example through daily actions that demonstrate they are deeply committed to their beliefs."[5] People who lead from the front set examples by spending time with their people, working side by side with colleagues, being visible during times of uncertainty and stress, asking questions, and listening carefully.

Provide Clear Direction

Leaders who are on the ground with their people, leading from the front, and setting the example are in the best position to make sure that everyone on their team or organization understands the direction they need to go in and pull together to achieve their objective.

General Gordon R. Sullivan, former Army Chief of Staff put it this way, "In an organization like ours, you have to think through what it is that you are becoming. Like a marathon runner, you have to get out in front, mentally, and pull the organization to you. You have to visualize the finish line—to see yourself there—and pull yourself along—not push—pull yourself to the future."[6]

An Army commander once said, "You must be seen to be heard." There's a great temptation for organizational leaders to rely exclusively on indirect leadership, to spread intent by issuing new policies, passing orders through subordinates or communicating electronically with people scattered far and wide. However, nothing can take the place of face-to-face contact, especially in setting direction. Good leaders make every effort to get out among their people. There they can spot-check intent to see that the mission is understood among those who must execute it.

Providing direction means not only setting a goal or objective, or describing a vision of the future but also inspiring people to pursue it with all their passion. To inspire people in this way, leaders must understand their people and speak their language. And this again requires leading from the front.

Effective leaders constantly observe, counsel, develop, teach, and listen; they know they must be just the kind of team player they want their subordinates to be—and more. Noel Tichy emphasizes the personal commitment effective leaders make to developing and teaching: "Winning companies win because they have leaders at all levels, and they have leaders at all levels because their top leaders make developing other leaders a priority. They personally devote enormous energy and time to teaching, and they encourage other leaders in the company to do the same."[7]

Build Morale and the Determination to Win

Morale, as we saw in Chapter Three, is how people feel about themselves, their team, and their leaders. We pointed out that high morale comes from good leadership, shared hardship, and mutual respect. Leading from the front—getting the right information, setting the example, inspiring people to pull together to achieve the objective—is a powerful and necessary tool for creating high morale.

What is it that carries soldiers through the terrible challenges of combat? It's the will to win, the ability to gut it out when things get really tough, even when things look hopeless. Army leaders understand the human dimension and anticipate soldiers' reactions to stress, especially to the tremendous stress of combat. In the Army, leaders who don't lead from the front cannot help their soldiers deal with stress and keep on going. (Soldiers are extremely sensitive to situations where their leaders are not at risk, and they're not likely to forget a mistake by a leader they haven't seen.) Leaders who are out with their soldiers—in the same rain or snow, under the same blazing sun or in the same dark night, under the same threat of enemy artillery or small-arms fire—can better motivate their soldiers to carry on under extreme conditions. And they find out the reality of the situation in a way that reports and analyses can never capture.

Of course, business and government organizations do not face the prospect of combat and the stress and fear that accompanies it. Yet people in many of these organizations do experience debilitating stress and fear—often produced by their own organizations, often produced by executives who hide behind memos and policies, who don't communicate, who don't want to listen, who, in short, don't lead from the front. When leaders don't lead from the front, the organization suffers: trust dissolves, rumors abound, new initiatives are resisted, people look out for themselves (because it's clear that their leaders aren't looking out for them), and fear reigns. These are all the hallmarks of terrible morale. In the military, this leads to defeat on the battlefield; in civilian organizations, this leads to defeat in the marketplace.

Leaders in all organizations need to plant the winning spirit in their people, the commitment to do their part to accomplish the mission, no matter when, no matter where, no matter what. Henry Mintzberg describes leading from the front as leadership that "does not sit on top and pronounce. It surrounds process, energizes, facilitates it, and infuses it by getting personally involved, so that people feel inspired to do good things."[8]

In sum, leading from the front involves these practices: being visible, moving about, going first, communicating directly, and most of all, putting yourself on the line. A real leader does not sit on the fence, waiting to see which way the wind is blowing. The leader articulates clear positions on issues affecting the organization and is the embodiment of the enterprise, of its values and principles. Because leading from the front is needed to build trust, maintain morale, and provide clear direction, it is essential in building and leading teams, the topic of the next chapter.

IT TAKES A TEAM

Success Through Teamwork

An article by Master Sergeant Emma Krouser in the March 27, 2003, edition of the *Army News Service* details that division's exploits during the first days of the Iraq war. The division traveled more than two hundred miles in about thirty-six hours with troops engaging enemy forces along the way in the initial ground assault.

"This is a lethal, lethal outfit," Brig. Gen. Lloyd Austin, assistant division commander, told Sgt. Krouser. "Once again these soldiers have proven they can do in the fight exactly what they have done in training. They don't hesitate—they don't blink."

"I think the division has been extremely successful, thus far," said Maj. Ross Coffman, division tactical command officer in charge. "We've accomplished all of our goals and we've met every mission the Corps put before us. We've done it faster and more successfully than anyone could ever imagine."

While in constant contact with enemy forces, the division was moving farther and faster than at any other time in recent history, according to Krouser. All the while, soldiers were continuing to maintain vehicles, personal weapons, and pushing food, fuel, and personnel to forward troop areas. "We've moved continuously for almost thirty-six hours, maintained where everybody was, control of who's doing what, and resourced the fight from our C2Vs as we were moving. That's an incredible capability," Austin said.

"The soldiers are taking care of each other, working hard, and staying focused. This is the best trained division in the United States Army and they will get the job done—no matter what," Austin said.[1]

Virtually every executive staff I've ever come across believes in teamwork. At least they say they do. Sadly, a scarce few of them make teamwork a reality in their organizations; in fact they often end up creating environments in which political infighting and departmental silos are the norm. . . . Before deciding that teamwork is the answer, ask these questions of yourself and your fellow team members:

- *Are we capable of admitting to mistakes, weaknesses, insufficient knowledge?*
- *Can we speak up openly when we disagree?*
- *Will we confront behavioral problems directly?*
- *Can we put the success of the team or organization over our own?*

Patrick M. Lencioni, "The Trouble with Teamwork,"
Leader to Leader, Summer 2002, 29

The 3rd Division's successful performance in Iraq obviously depended on superb teamwork. The division combined shared purpose and cohesive, disciplined teams to build the confidence and motivation necessary to fight and win in the face of uncertainty and adversity. Both leaders and soldiers understood that no plan remains intact after a unit crosses the line of departure. Advancing two hundred miles in thirty-six hours in hostile territory and adverse weather tested teamwork to the limit, and the 3rd Division passed the test with flying colors. In such life-and-death situations, superb teamwork in the Army isn't just desirable, it's a necessity.

The Army teaches that leadership is not a solo performance, but rather a team effort. A leader's job in the Army—or in any organization—isn't to make everyone the same but to take advantage of the fact that everyone is different and build a cohesive team. In the Army, being part of a team is not something laid on top of or in addition to one's other responsibilities; it is a fundamental part of the soldier's and the leader's job, a daily reality. Again and again *Army Leadership* stresses: "The Army can't function except as a team." Notice that the manual doesn't say the Army functions *best* as a team; it says the Army functions *only* as a team. Teamwork isn't something the Army strives for, as so many private companies do. Instead, it is a fundamental requirement, imbuing the Army's whole approach to organization and leadership. Here is what *Army Leadership* says about the critical role of teamwork in the Army:

> [Soldiers] work hard and fight tenaciously when they're well-trained and feel they're part of a good team. Collective confidence comes from winning under challenging and stressful conditions. People's sense of belonging comes from technical and tactical proficiency—as individuals and then collectively as a team—and the confidence they have in their peers and their leaders. As cohesive teams combine into a network, a team of teams, organizations work in harness with those on the left and right to fight as a whole. The balance among three good battalions is more important than having a single outstanding one. Following that philosophy necessarily affects resource allocation and task assignment.

Russ Moxley and John Alexander of the Center for Creative Leadership say, "We have learned from experience that work teams that learn to utilize the skills and gifts and energies of all team members fully can creatively and effectively accomplish the leadership tasks. Leadership can and does emerge from a team when differences are honored, assumptions are suspended, and the quality of inter-action is good. Synergy does produce better results than what any individual can accomplish alone."[2]

John Katzenbach describes teams as performance units: "a small group of people (typically fewer than ten) with complementary skills (working skills rather than organizational position) who are equally committed to the following: a clear, compelling performance purpose; a set of specific goals; a common working approach." According to Katzenbach, team members hold each other mutually accountable for each of these areas. Key to team performance is "peer- and self-disci-pline, as well as mutual respect among members."[3]

Developing teams takes hard work, patience, and quite a bit of interpersonal skill on the part of the leader, but it's a worthwhile investment. Good teams get the job done. People who are part of a good team complete the mission on time with the resources given them and a minimum of wasted effort; in combat, good teams are the most effective and take the fewest casualties. Good teams do the following:

- Put the good of the team first.

- Work together to accomplish the mission.

- Execute tasks thoroughly and quickly.

- Meet or exceed standards.

- Thrive on demanding challenges.

- Learn from their experiences and are proud of their accomplishments.

Requirements for Effective Teamwork

The Army realizes that team identity doesn't come about just because people take an oath or join an organization; leaders can't force a team to come together any more than a farmer can force a plant to grow. Rather, the team identity grows out of mutual respect among its members and trust between leaders and subordinates. That bond between leaders and subordinates likewise springs from mutual respect as well as from discipline. And it allows members to know that they are members of a team, not cogs in the machine. There are a number of essentials in building teams.

Trust

In Chapter Two, we discussed Army values in detail. These values—loyalty, duty, respect, selfless service, honor, integrity, and personal courage—are not only necessary for leadership but support teamwork. Army values are all important in building trust, the foundation of teamwork. Trust is so important in building teamwork that it cannot be overemphasized. Trust begins with action, when leaders demonstrate discipline and competence, and lead from the front. Over time, subordinates learn that leaders do what they say they'll do. Likewise, leaders learn to trust their subordinates. That connection, that mutual assurance, is the link that helps organizations accomplish the most difficult tasks.

Army units train together to build collective competence; trust is a product of that competence. Subordinates learn to trust their leaders if the leaders know how to do their jobs and act consistently—if they say what they mean and mean what they say. Trust also springs from the collective competence of the team. As the team becomes more experienced and enjoys more successes, it becomes more cohesive.

Communication

Leaders understand themselves, the mission, and the message. They owe it to their organization and their people to share as much as possible. People have to know what to do and why. At the most basic level, communication is the primary way that effective leaders show they care. If subordinates are to succeed and the organization is to move forward, then the leader must work hard at maintaining positive communication. If leaders encourage open dialogue, actively listen to all perspectives, and ensure that subordinate leaders and staff can have a forthright, open, and honest voice in the organization without fear of negative consequences, they foster communication at all levels. Leaders who communicate openly and genuinely reinforce team values send a message of trust to subordinates and benefit from subordinates' good ideas. Trust and communication reinforce each other.

Persuasion is a communication skill important to leaders. Well-developed skills of persuasion and openness to working through controversy in a positive way help leaders overcome resistance and build support. These characteristics are particularly important in dealing with other leaders. By reducing grounds for misunderstanding, persuasion reduces time wasted in overcoming unimportant issues. It also ensures involvement of others, opens communication with them, and places value on their opinions—all team-building actions. Openness to discussing one's position and a positive attitude toward a dissenting view often diffuse tension and save time and resistance in the long run. By demonstrating these traits, effective leaders also provide an example that subordinates can use in self-development.

At all levels, leaders build teams by keeping team members informed. They share information, solicit input, and consider suggestions. This give-and-take also allows subordinates a glimpse into the mind of their leaders, which helps them prepare for the day when they will fill that job. The leader who sends these messages— "I value your opinion; you're part of the team; I'm preparing you for greater responsibilities"—strengthens the bonds that hold the team together.

Loyalty

In the Army, all soldiers are members of the same team, and they are loyal to one another and to the team. Just how important is it that people have a sense of the team? In the Army, it is essential.

The nation's cause, the purpose of the mission, and all the larger concerns may not be visible from a foxhole on the battlefield. Regardless of other issues, soldiers perform for the other people in the squad or section, for others in the team or crew, for the person on their right or left. This is a fundamental truth: soldiers perform because they don't want to let their buddies down.

People will do the most extraordinary things for their buddies. The job of Army leaders is to pull each member into the team because someday they may ask that person for extraordinary effort. Team building involves applying interpersonal leader skills that transform individuals into productive teams. If the leader has done the work, the team member won't let others down.

Selfless Service

Selfless service goes hand in hand with loyalty and is an essential component of teamwork. Team members give of themselves so that the team may succeed. In combat, some soldiers give themselves completely so that their comrades can live and the mission can be accomplished. But the need for selflessness isn't limited to combat situations. Requirements for individuals to place their own needs below those of their organization can occur during peacetime as well. And the requirement for selflessness doesn't decrease as one's rank or position in the organization rises; it increases.

Respect

Respect is another value that is an essential component for the development of disciplined, cohesive, and effective warfighting teams. In the deadly confusion of combat, soldiers often overcome incredible odds to accomplish the mission and protect the lives of their comrades. This spirit of selfless service and duty is built on a soldier's personal trust and respect for fellow soldiers. Discrimination and harassment, of course, destroys respect, and the Army works hard to combat discrimination and harassment in any form. But respect goes beyond issues of discrimination and harassment; it includes the broader issue of civility, the way people treat each other and those they come in contact with. It involves being sensitive to diversity and one's own behaviors that others may find insensitive, offensive, or abusive. Soldiers at all levels from buck privates to four-star generals treat everyone with dignity and respect.

Discipline

"Discipline brings pride to the unit," a company commander in Desert Storm said. "Discipline coupled with tough, realistic training is the key to high morale in units. Soldiers want to belong to good outfits, and our job as leaders is to give them the best outfit we can."

Discipline is, of course, essential in wartime. Disciplined soldiers and teams will continue to fight when the radios are jammed, when the plan falls apart, when the enemy does something unexpected. One sergeant major has described discipline as "a moral, mental, and physical state in which all ranks respond to the will of the leader, *whether he is there or not.*" Disciplined people take the right action, even if they don't feel like it. True discipline demands habitual and reasoned obedience, an obedience that preserves initiative and works, even when the leader isn't around. Soldiers and civilians who understand the purpose of the mission, trust the leader, and share Army values will do the right thing because they're truly committed to the organization.

In the Army, the highest form of discipline is achieved when people trust their leaders, understand and believe in the mission's purpose, value the team and their place in it, and have the will to see the mission through. This form of discipline produces individuals and teams who—in the really tough moments—come up with solutions themselves. Discipline and shared hardship pull people together in powerful ways. When people are part of a disciplined and cohesive team, they gain proficiency, are motivated, and willingly subordinate themselves to organizational needs. People who sense they're part of a competent, well-trained team act upon what the team needs; they're confident in themselves and feel a part of something important and compelling. These team members know that what they do matters and discipline themselves.

Discipline doesn't just mean barking orders and demanding an instant response—it's more complex than that. Disciplined leaders with strong values develop disciplined soldiers with strong values. Together they become disciplined, cohesive units that train hard, fight honorably, and win decisively. Major General John M. Schofield, in an address to the United States Corps of Cadets in 1879, explained:

> The discipline which makes the soldiers of a free country reliable in battle is not to be gained by harsh or tyrannical treatment. On the contrary, such treatment is far more likely to destroy than to make an army. It is possible to impart instruction and to give commands in such a manner and such a tone of voice to inspire in the soldier no feeling but an intense desire to obey, while the opposite manner and tone of voice cannot fail to excite strong resentment and a desire to disobey. The one mode or the other of dealing with subordinates springs from a corresponding spirit in the breast of the commander. He who feels the respect which is due to others cannot fail to inspire in them regard for himself, while he who feels, and hence manifests, disrespect toward others, especially his inferiors, cannot fail to inspire hatred against himself.

In the Army, leaders build discipline by training, using rewards and punishment judiciously, instilling confidence in, and building trust among team members, and creating a knowledgeable collective will. The confidence, trust, and collective will of a disciplined, cohesive unit is crucial in combat.

Team Building

Teams don't come together by accident, the Army realizes. Leaders must build and guide them through a series of developmental stages: formation, enrichment, and sustainment. Exhibit 5.1, taken from

Exhibit 5.1. Team-Building Stages

Formation Stage	Subordinate Challenges	Leader and Unit-Organization Actions
Generic	• Achieve belonging and acceptance. • Set personal and family concerns. • Learn about leaders and other members.	• Listen to and care for subordinates. • Design effective reception and orientation. • Communicate. • Reward positive contributions. • Set example.
Soldier critical	• Face the uncertainty of war. • Cope with fear of unknown injury and death. • Adjust to sights and sounds of war. • Adjust to separation from home and family.	• Talk with each soldier. • Reassure with calm presence. • Communicate vital safety tips. • Provide stable situation. • Establish buddy system. • Assist soldiers in dealing with immediate problems.
Enrichment stage Generic	• Trust leaders and other members. • Find close friends. • Learn who is in charge. • Accept the way things are done. • Adjust to feelings about how things ought to be done. • Overcome family versus unit conflict.	• Trust and encourage trust. • Allow growth while keeping control. • Identify and channel emerging leaders. • Establish clear lines of authority. • Establish individual and unit goals. • Train as a unit for mission. • Build pride through accomplishment. • Acquire self-evaluation/self-assessment habits. • Be fair and give responsibility.
Soldier critical	• Survive. • Demonstrate competence. • Become a team member quickly. • Learn about the enemy. • Learn about the battlefield. • Avoid life-threatening mistakes.	• Train as a unit for combat. • Demonstrate competence. • Know the soldiers. • Pace subordinate battlefield integration. • Provide stable unit climate. • Emphasize safety awareness for improved readiness.
Sustainment stage Generic	• Trust others. • Share ideas and feelings freely. • Assist other team members. • Sustain trust and confidence. • Share mission and values.	• Demonstrate trust. • Focus on teamwork, training, and maintaining. • Respond to subordinate problems. • Devise more challenging training. • Build pride and spirit through unit sports and social and spiritual activities.
Soldier critical	• Adjust to continuous operations. • Cope with casualties. • Adjust to enemy actions. • Overcome boredom. • Avoid rumors. • Control fear, anger, despair, and panic.	• Observe and enforce sleep discipline. • Sustain safety awareness. • Inform soldiers. • Know and deal with soldiers' perceptions. • Keep soldiers productively busy. • Use In Process Reviews (IPRs) and After Action Reviews (AARs). • Act decisively in face of panic.

Source: Army Leadership (FM-100), pp. 5–21.

Army Leadership, may make the process seem more orderly than it actually is; as with so many things leaders do, the reality is more complicated than the explanation. Army leaders know that each team develops differently: the boundaries between stages are not hard and fast. Leaders must be sensitive to the characteristics of the team they're building and of its individual members.

Teams, like individuals, have different personalities. As with individuals, the leader's job isn't to make teams that are clones of one another but to make best use of the particular talents of the team, maximize the potential of the unit climate, and motivate aggressive execution.

Formation Stage

Team building begins with receiving new members; everyone knows how important first impressions are when meeting someone new. The same thing is true of teams; the new member's reception and orientation create that crucial first impression that colors the person's opinion of the team for a long time. A good experience joining the organization will make it easier for the new member to fit in and contribute. Even in peacetime, the way a person is received into an organization can have long-lasting effects—good or bad—on the individual and the team. Teams work best when new members are brought onboard quickly, when they're made to feel a part of the team.

Reception is the leader's welcome; the orientation begins with meeting other team members, learning the layout of the workplace, learning the schedule and other requirements, and generally getting to know the lay of the land. In combat, leaders may not have time to spend with new members. In this case, new arrivals are often assigned a buddy who will help them get oriented and keep them out of trouble until they learn their way around. The two steps—reception and orientation—are dramatically different in peace and war. In combat, this sponsorship process can literally mean life or death to new members and to the team.

Enrichment Stage

New teams and new team members gradually move from questioning everything to trusting themselves, their peers, and their leaders. Leaders earn that trust by listening, following up on what they hear, establishing clear lines of authority, and setting standards. In the Army, by far the most important thing a leader does to strengthen the team is training. Training takes a group of individuals and molds them into a team while preparing them to accomplish their tasks and the team objective. Training occurs during all three team-building stages, but is particularly important during enrichment; it's at this point that the team is building collective proficiency.

Sustainment Stage

When a team reaches this stage, its members think of the team as "their team." They own it, have pride in it, and want it to succeed. At this stage, team members will do what needs to be done without being told. Every new mission gives the leader a chance to make the bonds even stronger, to challenge the team to reach for new heights. The leader develops his subordinates because they're tomorrow's team leaders. He continues to train the team so that it maintains proficiency in the collective and individual tasks it must perform to accomplish its missions. Finally, the Army leader works to keep the team going in spite of the stresses and losses of combat.

Within a larger team, smaller teams may be at different stages of development. For instance, members of one squad may be used to working together. They trust one another and get the job done—usually exceeding the standard—with no wasted motion. A second squad in the same platoon just received three new soldiers and a team leader from another company. As a team, the second squad is less mature; it will take them some time to get up to the level of the first squad. New team members have to learn how things work: they have to be brought onboard and made to feel they are members of the team; they must learn the standards and the climate of their new unit; they'll have to demonstrate some competence before other members really accept them; and finally, they must practice working together. Leaders, who must oversee all this, are better equipped if they know what to expect.

Leading Teams

Exhibit 5.1 shows the things Army leaders are taught to do to pull a team together, get it going in the right direction, and keep it moving. But that list only hints at the work that lies ahead as one faces the ongoing task of leading a team.

In his book *Leading Teams*, J. Richard Hackman identifies effective coaching as critical for team performance. And as we have seen, the Army encourages leaders to constantly observe, counsel, develop, and listen. Leaders must be every bit the team player they want their subordinates to be—and more.

Leaders work consistently to create individual and team ownership of organizational goals. By knowing their subordinates—their aspirations, fears, and concerns—leaders can ensure that their subordinate organizations and leaders work together. Taking time to allow subordinates to develop ways to meet organizational missions fosters ownership of a plan. Providing processes in which subordinate organizations define supporting tasks and suggest the training required to gain and maintain proficiency is an example of a process that encourages collective investment in training. This investment leads to a commitment that not only supports execution but also reduces the chances of internal conflict.

As we have seen, effective leaders provide clear direction to their teams. With clearly communicated purpose and direction, subordinates can then determine what they must do and why. Within that broad framework, leaders give power to subordinates, delegating authority to act within the intent: "Here's where we're headed, why we're going there, and how we're going to get there." Purpose and direction align the efforts of subordinates working toward common goals. The Army understands that people want direction. They want to be given challenging tasks, training in how to accomplish them, and the resources necessary to do them well. Then they want to be left alone to do the job. If the leaders of the small teams that make up the Army are competent, and if their members trust one another, those teams and the larger team of teams will work together and get the job done.

Successful leaders create a positive climate for their team. People who belong to successful teams look at nearly everything in a positive light; their winner attitudes are infectious and they see problems as challenges rather than obstacles. Research shows that when people are angry, anxious, alienated, or depressed, their work suffers. They can't think as clearly; they can't take in information as fully, understand it as deeply, and respond as adaptively when the organizational climate is poor. A climate that promotes strong values encourages learning and promotes creative performance. The foundation for a positive organizational climate is a healthy ethical climate, but that alone is insufficient. Characteristics of successful organizational climates include a clear, widely known intent; well-trained and confident people; disciplined, cohesive teams; and trusted, competent leadership.

To create such a climate, leaders recognize mistakes as opportunities to learn and reward character and competence. Leaders value honest feedback and constantly use all available means to maintain a feel for the environment, such as town hall meetings, surveys, and councils. And of course, personal observation brings leaders face-to-face with the people affected by their decisions and policies. A leader's consistent, sincere effort to see what's really going on and fix things that are not working right can result in mutual respect throughout his or her organization.

Ethics is a critical ingredient in organizational climate. Army leaders are expected to be ethical standard-bearers for their teams. They are responsible for building an ethical climate that demands and rewards behavior consistent with Army values. The Army provides support for leaders in building an ethical climate—for example, the chaplain, staff judge advocate, inspector general, and equal opportunity employment manager—to assist them in building and assessing their organization's ethical climate, but the ultimate responsibility belongs to the leader.

Just because a leader sets a good ethical example doesn't necessarily mean subordinates will follow it. Some of them may feel that circumstances justify unethical behavior. Therefore, leaders must constantly pay careful attention to the team's current ethical climate and take prompt action to correct any discrepancies between it and the highest standards.

Effective leaders build cohesive organizations. A cohesive team accomplishes the mission much more efficiently than a group of individuals. Just as a football team practices to win on the gridiron, so must a team of soldiers practice to be effective on the battlefield. And effective leaders overcome, and even capitalize on, diversity of background and experience to create the energy necessary to achieve organizational goals. They resolve conflicts among subordinate leaders as well as any conflicts between their own organization and others. For example, subordinate leaders may compete for limited resources while pursuing their individual organization's goals. Two battalion commanders may both want and need a certain maneuver training area to prepare for deployment, so they both present the issue professionally and creatively to their commander. The brigade commander must then weigh and decide between the different unit requirements, balancing their competing demands with the greater good of the entire organization and the Army. Yet an even better situation is if the organizational climate facilitates teamwork and cooperation that results in the subordinate commanders themselves producing a satisfactory solution.

Effective leaders emphasize teamwork and cooperation over competition. They communicate their intent so subordinates can accomplish the mission, no matter what happens to the original plan. Because organizational leaders primarily work through subordinates, empowerment and delegation are indispensable. As a result of communicating with subordinates, listening to their responses, and obtaining feedback from their assessments, leaders are better equipped to make decisions.

Following up is an important part of team leadership: Does the team understand the tasks? Is the team taking the necessary actions to complete them? Check the chain of command again: Does everyone have the word? Leader involvement in this follow-up validates the priorities and demonstrates that the leader is serious about seeing the mission completed. Leaders who fail to follow up send a message that the priorities are not really that important and their orders are not really binding.

The Challenge of Diversity

There is great diversity in the Army. At the end of 1999, the Army was 59.2 percent white, 26.5 percent African American, 7.6 percent Hispanic, and 6.7 percent other ethnic groups. The members of the Army community represented over 150 religious groups. They were men and women. Some were married, and some were single. Some had children, some did not. They were on active duty and in reserve components. Most had high school diplomas, some had GEDs. Some had a little college, and some had one or more degrees. They ranged in age from seventeen to sixty-five. They were a reflection of the people we see around us every day—a reflection of America.

Numerous articles and news reports have portrayed the Army as one of the most successful organizations—if not *the* most successful organization—in bringing together people from diverse backgrounds to forge a caring and respectful community. How does the Army do it? In forging cohesive teams, the best Army leaders do not try to "manage" this diversity but rather embrace and respect it. As America becomes ever more diverse, Army leaders are taught to be aware that they will deal with people from a wider range of ethnic, racial, and religious backgrounds. They are expected to appreciate beliefs different from their own as long as those beliefs don't conflict with Army values, are not illegal, and are not unethical. They are encouraged to actively seek out opportunities to learn about people and cultures different from their own. It shows respect to seek to understand other people's background, see things from their perspective, and appreciate what's important to them.

Respect—there is that word again. More than a word, it is a critical Army value, and it underlies the Army's approach to our increasingly diverse society. Respect for the individual forms the basis for the rule of law, the very essence of what makes America. In the Army, respect means recognizing and appreciating the inherent dignity and worth of all people. Army leaders honor everyone's individual worth by treating all people with dignity and respect.

Respect is also an essential component for the development of disciplined, cohesive, and effective warfighting teams. A leader's willingness to tolerate discrimination or harassment on any basis, or a failure to cultivate a climate of respect, eats away at trust and erodes unit cohesion.

Respect for diversity is not only important at the squad or platoon level. During World War II, one of General Eisenhower's duties as Supreme Allied Commander in the European Theater of Operations was to form his theater headquarters, the Supreme Headquarters of the Allied Expeditionary Force. Eisenhower had to create an environment in this multinational headquarters in which staff members from the different Allied armies could work together harmoniously. It was one of Eisenhower's toughest jobs.

The forces under his command—American, British, French, Canadian, and Polish—brought not only different languages but different ways of thinking, different ideas about what was important, and different strategies. Eisenhower could have tried to bend everyone to his will and his way of thinking; he was the boss, after all. But it's doubtful the Allies would have fought as well for a bullying commander or that a bullying commander would have survived politically. Instead, he created a positive organizational climate that made best use of the various capabilities of his subordinates. This kind of work takes tact, patience, trust—and respect. It doesn't destroy existing cultures but creates a new one.

Lessons for Civilian Organizations

As anyone who has spent much time in the corporate world knows, there are hundreds of training firms offering team-building programs. They will take your group out to climb ropes and get lost in the woods. They will give everyone personality assessments and assign personality "types"—introverted, extroverted, and so on. There are team-building exercises and assessments galore. And don't get us wrong; these can be useful in the right situation. But to our way of thinking, many go right past what the Army has recognized so well: values underlie teamwork. Values come first, and behavior follows.

Organizations that want to promote teamwork cannot do so if they do not also support the underlying values that support teamwork. Army values of loyalty, duty, respect, selfless service, honor, integrity, and personal courage clearly support teamwork. But there is another aspect of the Army's value system that is tremendously effective in building teamwork. The heroic bravery of the soldiers in Mogadishu described at the opening of Chapter Two (and portrayed in the movie *Blackhawk Down*) was not only a spectacular example of the power of teamwork, but a clear illustration of the Army's imperative, "Leave no soldier behind." Though not formally a part of the Army's training on team leadership, the Army's famous dictum to leave no soldier behind is a clear consequence of the value of loyalty and a critical component of the Army's team ethos—an ethos that is entirely absent in too many civilian organizations.

Of course, in a civilian organization, employees do not get captured behind enemy lines, but they do fall behind, go off course, and fail. And too often, those around them think that such failure is a personal problem on the part of the employee, not a team problem. Such an attitude shows little loyalty and is antithetical to teamwork.

Contrast that approach to the approach used at DPR Construction, as explained in *Fast Company* magazine. At DPR "we have chosen to be collaborative rather than combative," says a member of the management team. "And that means that we don't allow other members of our team to fail."[4]

Remember the words of Patrick Lencioni, a leading management consultant we quoted at the beginning of this chapter: "Virtually every executive staff I've ever come across believes in teamwork. At least they say they do. Sadly, a scarce few of them make teamwork a reality in their organizations; in fact they often end up creating environments where political infighting and departmental silos are the norm. And yet they continue to tout their belief in teamwork, as if that alone will somehow make it magically appear."[5] Examine the climate in your organization. Does it promote individual initiative over teamwork, competition over collaboration? If so, you probably need to work hard to redefine your values or accept that you cannot become a team-based organization.

Lencioni, the author of *The Five Dysfunctions of a Team*, says that there are five building blocks to successful teams: vulnerability-based trust, healthy conflict, unwavering commitment, unapologetic accountability, and collective orientation to results. None of these work if people's values and behavior won't support them.

We have to keep our egos in check, place the team ahead of personal gain, be open to admitting to ignorance and mistakes, speak up and constructively criticize when we disagree, and hold each other accountable.

Noel Tichy, author of *The Leadership Engine* and *The Cycle of Leadership*, echoes Lencioni: "You would think that the top leaders of major institutions would relish the opportunity to work together, setting an agenda for the future of their institutions. But in every group there are always resisters, people who don't want to join the game and, often, who don't want the game to take place at all. In each of these instances, the process has gone ahead and worked only when the senior leaders have firmly taken command."[6]

When teams fail, the blame is usually placed on lack of commitment to the team's task and goals, or to office politics. In our experience, these are just symptoms of the deeper problem of the organization's values being inimical to real teamwork. Orpheus, the world's only leaderless orchestra, takes a unique team approach to managing itself. It has no conductor, so every member is responsible for making the orchestra—the team—work. The values Orpheus promotes are telling. As explained by Harvey Seifter and Peter Economy in their book, *Leadership Ensemble*, the members of Orpheus know that communication is the lifeblood of the organization. Whether or not they agree with what is being said, Orpheus members are expected to listen to one another's views, and to respect what is said and the person who said it. They are also expected to contribute their views. But there is a right time and a wrong time to talk. According to an Orpheus violinist, there are times when they are practicing a piece and it isn't working and "everybody can feel what's wrong—but do you have a solution? Do you know how to solve a problem?" No topic is considered out of bounds for the members of the group, and constructive criticism is always welcome. In Orpheus, two-way communication is expected, fostered, and reinforced almost constantly.[7]

As James Collins and Jerry Porras argue in *Built to Last*, "the success of visionary companies—at least in part—[comes] from underlying processes and fundamental dynamics embedded in the organization and not primarily [from] a single great idea or some great, all-knowing, godlike visionary who made great decisions, and had great charisma, and led with great authority."[8] A critical part of the fundamental dynamics needed is effective teamwork.

Finally, leaders everywhere need to adopt the Army's approach and embrace and celebrate diversity in building their teams and organizations. Resisting the temptation to deny reality, and daring to define the new realities, may be a leader's greatest challenges. The challenges we confront today are numerous and daunting, but perhaps the most pressing are the demographic shifts that are reshaping Western society. Given the growing impact of these changes on our society and its institutions, our ability to see the remarkable opportunities in the growing diversity—not trying to "manage" it—may decide the future of our organizations.

If we fail on the key challenge of equal access to opportunity, our efforts in every other realm may falter. It does little good to formulate a brilliant competitive strategy unless we include the people inside the organization who must carry it out and the people in the marketplace and the community who form a large part of the customer base. To further our mission and build the richly diverse organization, we must make inclusion and participation top priorities.

We cannot ensure equal access or build upon our diverse strengths by sitting at our desks and proclaiming, "Let there be diversity!" Rather, we must scan the environment and gather current and credible information about our workforce, our boards, our customers, and our communities. Understanding our constituents' demographics is key to meeting their needs, and to creating conditions in which the rich diversity of the organization brings new vitality to the workplace and to our neighborhoods.

Only with such understanding can our leadership teams hold before the people of the organization a vision of the future. For our most effective organizations, that vision will include a richly diverse organization with governance, management, and the workforce representative of the whole community. Leaders of these organizations know it takes committed, energetic, and able people in cohesive teams to serve present and future customers who are the changing community.

MANAGING COMPLEXITY, LEADING CHANGE

Army's "Digitized Division" Wages First Combat

By Gary Sheftick

BAGHDAD, Iraq (Army News Service, April 17, 2003)—Elements of the 4th Infantry Division battled Iraqi paramilitary fighters yesterday at al Taji airfield, north of Baghdad, in the division's first combat since it became the Army's "experimental force" in 1995.

Now known as the "digitized division" because of its tactical Internet and high-tech systems in each armored vehicle, the 4th ID crossed into Iraq Sunday from Kuwait. After 40 hours rolling north, the division passed through Baghdad Tuesday night and its leading elements stopped near al Taji airfield.

Wednesday morning soldiers of the division's 1st Brigade spotted paramilitary troops loading ammunition into a civilian vehicle on the air base. In a firefight that ensued, 4th ID soldiers killed and wounded a number of Iraqis and captured more than 100 enemy fighters, according to a U.S. Central Command report.

"The enemy force also had unmanned artillery pieces, armored personnel carriers, and loaded multiple rocket launcher systems, a surface-to-air-missile warehouse, and some computers," said Brig. Gen. Vincent Brooks. The 4th ID soldiers also destroyed some T-72 tanks at the airfield, Brooks said.

The 4th ID from Fort Hood, Texas, deployed to the CENTCOM theater earlier this month. Its M1 tanks and advanced Bradleys were reportedly in ships off the coast of Turkey for about a month, but in the end the equipment was off-loaded in Kuwait.

That equipment included new digitized systems such as the Force XXI Battle Command Brigade and Below, [which] allows a soldier to know where he is, where his buddy is, and where the enemy is.

When the 4th ID became the Army's experimental force in 1995, its 1st Brigade became Task Force XXI and was outfitted with digital communications systems, new equipment, and new weapons systems. In March 1997, after training on the new equipment and new tactics, the 1st Brigade was tested in an advanced warfighting experiment at the National Training Center, Fort Irwin, Calif. Its success against NTC's world-class Opposing Force was largely attributed to increased situational awareness made possible by digital communications.

In the largest rotation ever at NTC, the 4th Infantry Division demonstrated its most recent digitized systems beginning March 31 to April 14, 2001. The Division Capstone Exercise at NTC was the Army's first look at the 4th ID's elite mechanized and aviation warfighting capability, including its FBCB2, under realistic battlefield conditions, officials said.

> *Battles during the [exercise] demonstrated that*
> *Army Battle Command Systems—commonly re-*
> *ferred to as digital information systems or ABCS—*
> *were able to empower soldiers to "move more quickly*
> *over the extended battlespace," said Brig. Gen. James*
> *D. Thurman, who then commanded NTC. Now the*
> *division is employing those digital information systems*
> *in an actual combat zone.*
> *[http://www4.army.mil/ocpa/read.php?story_id_key=220]*

The history of the post-Vietnam Army illustrates how strategic leaders' commitment can shape the environment and harness change to improve the institution while continuing to operate effectively. The Army began seeking only volunteers in the early 1970s. With the all-volunteer force came a tremendous emphasis on new doctrinal, personnel, and training initiatives that took years to mature. The Army tackled problems in drug abuse, racial tensions, and education with ambitious, long-range plans and aggressive leadership actions. Strategic leaders overhauled doctrine and created an environment that improved training at all levels; the combat training center program provided a uniform, rock-solid foundation of a single, well-understood warfighting doctrine upon which to build a trained and ready Army. Simultaneously, new equipment, weapons, vehicles, and uniforms were introduced. The result was the Army of Desert Storm, which differed greatly from the force of fifteen years before.

None of these changes happened by chance or evolution. Change depended on the hard work of direct and organizational leaders who developed systematically in an environment directed, engineered, and led by strategic leaders.

All organizations face changes from new technologies, shifts in the workforce, new competitive threats and opportunities, and a host of other factors. Leaders can either react to change, making adjustments to keep their balance as the waves of change tip the organization this way and that—or they can proactively lead change, anticipating and taking advantage of new trends and developments. The Army has no choice but to face change and lead. It's in a nearly constant state of flux, with new people, new missions, new technologies, new equipment, and new information. At the same time, the Army, inspired by its leaders, must innovate and create change. The Army's customs, procedures, structure, and sheer size make change especially daunting and stressful. Nonetheless, the Army must be flexible enough to produce and respond to change, even as it preserves the core of traditions that tie it to the nation, its heritage, and its values. In this chapter, we first discuss one of the Army's greatest change leaders, General George C. Marshall, and then present guidelines and tools for leading change.

General George C. Marshall

General George C. Marshall (1880–1959) was one of the greatest strategic leaders of World War II and of the twentieth century. Marshall first distinguished himself as a staff officer in World War I. After varied tasks, including service in China in the 1920s, he headed the Army as Chief of Staff from 1939 to 1945, having been chosen over thirty-four officers senior to him, and became General of the Army (five-star general) in December 1944. After the war, he was Secretary of State from 1947 to 1949, Secretary of Defense from 1950 to 1951, and winner of the Nobel Peace Prize in 1953. His example over many years demonstrates the skills and actions that are the hallmarks of strategic leadership, an exemplar of how to lead change.

When Marshall became Army Chief of Staff in 1939, he knew that he had a lot to learn. He wrote: "It became clear to me that at the age of fifty-eight, I would have to learn new tricks that were not taught in the military manuals or on the battlefield. In this position I am a political soldier and will have to put my training in rapping-out orders and making snap decisions on the back burner, and have to learn the arts of persuasion and guile. I must become an expert in a whole new set of skills."[1] He also knew he faced a monumental change effort. He had to waken the Army from its interwar slumber and grow it beyond its 174,000 soldiers—a size that ranked it seventeenth internationally, behind Bulgaria and Portugal. By 1941 he had begun to move the Army toward his vision of what it needed to become: a world-changing force of 8,795,000 soldiers and airmen. His vision was remarkably accurate: by the end of the war, eighty-nine divisions and over 8,200,000 soldiers in U.S. Army uniforms had made history.

Marshall wanted to reach deep within the Army for leaders capable of the conceptual leaps necessary to fight the impending war. He lobbied Congress to change the rules of promotion so that promising officers, regardless of seniority, could be promoted. He demanded leaders ready for the huge tasks ahead, and he accepted no excuses. As he found colonels, lieutenant colonels, and even majors who seemed ready for the biggest challenge of their lives, he promoted them ahead of those more senior but less capable and made many of them generals. Among his protégés were Dwight D. Eisenhower, Omar Bradley, Mark Clark, and Joseph Stilwell. For generals who could not adjust to the sweeping changes in the Army, he made career shifts as well: he retired them. His loyalty to the institution and the nation came before any personal relationships.

Merely assembling the required number of soldiers would not be enough. Mobilizing these troops to the European and Pacific theaters—along with the supporting materials of guns, ammunition, boots, food, and medicine—required massive innovation in global distribution channels. In addition, the mass Army that was forming required a new structure to manage the forces and resources the nation was mobilizing for the war effort. Realizing this, Marshall reorganized the Army into the Army Ground Forces, Army Air Forces, and Army Service Forces. His foresight organized the Army for the evolving nature of warfare.

Preparing for combat required more than manning the force. Marshall understood that World War I had presented confusing lessons about the future of warfare. Based on his experience during that war and later reflection, study, and analysis, he distilled a vision of the future. He believed that maneuver of motorized formations spearheaded by tanks and supported logistically by trucks (instead of horse-drawn wagons) would replace the almost siegelike battles of World War I. So while the French trusted the immovable Maginot Line, Marshall emphasized the new technologies that would heighten the speed and complexity of the coming conflict.

Further, Marshall championed commonsense training to prepare soldiers to go overseas ready to fight and win. By having new units spend sufficient time on marksmanship, fitness, drill, and fieldcraft, he ensured that soldiers and leaders had the requisite competence and confidence to face an experienced enemy.

Before and during the war, Marshall showed a gift for communicating with the American public. He worked closely with the press, frequently confiding in senior newsmen so they would know about the Army's activities and the progress of the war. They responded to his trust by not printing damaging or premature stories. His relaxed manner and complete command of pertinent facts reassured the press, and through it the nation, that America's youth were entrusted to the right person.

He was equally successful with Congress. Marshall understood that getting what he wanted meant asking, not demanding. His humble and respectful approach with lawmakers won his troops what they needed. Because he never sought anything for himself (his five-star rank was awarded over his objections), his credibility soared.

However, Marshall knew how to shift his approach depending on the audience, the environment, and the situation. He refused to be intimidated by leaders such as Prime Minister Winston Churchill,

Secretary of War Henry Stimson, or even the president. Though he was always respectful, his integrity demanded that he stand up for his deeply held convictions—and he did, without exception. Soldiers above and below him in rank knew that Marshall would not lie, cheat, or steal or tolerate those who did. Marshall had also thought about his own weaknesses as a soldier and leader; he was a master at picking subordinates to compensate for those weaknesses, not "yes men" who only said what they thought the boss wanted to hear.

The U.S. role in Europe was to open a major second front to relieve pressure on the Soviet Union and ensure the Allied victory over Germany. Marshall had spent years preparing the Army for Operation Overlord, the D-Day invasion that would become the main effort by the Western Allies and the one expected to lead to final victory over Nazi Germany. Many assumed Marshall would command it. President Roosevelt might have felt obligated to reward the general's faithful and towering service, but Marshall never raised the subject. Ultimately, the president told Marshall that it was more important that he lead global resourcing than command a theater of war. Eisenhower got the command, while Marshall continued to serve on staff. And there, as Army Chief of Staff, Marshall served with unsurpassed vision and brilliance, engineering the greatest victory in our nation's history and setting an extraordinary example for those who came after him.

Marshall understood that the real object of war is to prepare for peace. In his June 5, 1947, speech at Harvard University, he announced a daring plan for the reconstruction of Europe, including Germany, which became known as the Marshall Plan. "Our policy is directed not against any country or doctrine but against hunger, poverty, desperation, and chaos," Marshall said. "Its purpose should be the revival of a working economy in the world so as to permit the emergence of political and social conditions in which free institutions can exist."[2] For this European reconstruction plan effort, George C. Marshall was awarded the Nobel Prize for peace in 1953, the first soldier ever to receive that honor.

> *"Our policy is directed not against any country or doctrine but against hunger, poverty, desperation, and chaos."*
>
> General George C. Marshall

The Challenge of Change

George C. Marshall stands out as an exemplary leader during times of great change. Of course, in the more than two centuries of its history, the Army has gone through major change generation after generation. Red-coated troops no longer march shoulder to shoulder against a line of musket fire. Cavalry regiments no longer ride horses, but use armored vehicles. Precision strikes have replaced carpet bombing.

Change never ends. Indeed, it is accelerating. The changing nature of the world environment will have a huge impact on Army leadership in the near future. For the Army, the twenty-first century began in 1989 with the fall of the Berlin Wall and subsequent collapse of the Soviet Union. America no longer defines its security interests in terms of a single major threat. Instead, it faces numerous smaller threats and situations, any of which can quickly mushroom into a major security challenge. At one end of the spectrum, creative and adaptive opponents will employ strategies to destroy U.S. resolve by attacking our homeland, killing innocent civilians, and conducting prolonged operations. Some will immerse themselves in our culture, exploit our vulnerabilities, and seek to create maximum fear in the hearts of our citizens and coalition partners. They will seek to fracture confidence in public institutions, generate economic uncertainty, and divide the focus as well as the will of the general public. Respecting the superior power of U.S. military forces, they will employ anti-access strategies comprising several integrated lines of action (from diplomacy to information operations to direct and indirect military actions) aimed at preventing or limiting U.S. impact on regional crises.

And since the end of the Cold War, the Army has seen tremendous organizational changes—dramatic decreases in the number of soldiers and Department of the Army civilians in all components, changes in assignment policies, base closings, and a host of other shifts that put stress on soldiers, civilians, and families. During those same years, the number of deployments to support missions such as peace operations and nation assistance has increased. At the same time, Army leaders have had to prepare their soldiers for the stresses of combat, the ultimate change-driver, in Afghanistan and twice in Iraq.

Clearly, the industrial revolution transformed society and the ways and means by which warfare was conducted in the nineteenth and twentieth centuries. Now, the information revolution, with the promise of accelerating breakthroughs for surveilling, understanding, and communicating is expected to create a base of knowledge for military planning and execution unprecedented in scope, volume, accuracy, and timeliness. Although the requirement for information superiority is not a new concept, information technologies make this simpler and easier, and therefore more powerful, than ever before.

Technological advances have also had a great impact on the Army and its people. Military leaders have always had to deal with the effect of technological changes. What's different today is the rate at which technology, including warfighting technology, is changing. Rapid advances in new technologies are forcing the Army to change many aspects of the way it operates and are creating new leadership challenges. As witnessed by the latest war in Iraq, the Army is meeting these challenges successfully.

Emerging combat, combat support, and combat service support technologies bring more than changes to doctrine. Technological change allows organizations to do the things they do now better and faster, but it also enables them to do things that were not possible before. So a part of leveraging technology is envisioning the future capability that could be exploited by developing a technology. Another aspect is rethinking the form the organization ought to take in order to exploit new processes that previously were not available. This is why strategic leaders take time to think "beyond the walls."

The Army has developed a concept to describe the twenty-first-century world of increasing and changing complexity: VUCA. VUCA is actually an acronym for the words volatility, uncertainty, complexity, and ambiguity.

- *Volatility because change today is not gradual and predictable, but discontinuous and surprising.* Army leaders operate in a volatile environment. Change may arrive suddenly and unannounced. As they plan for contingencies, the Army's strategic leaders prepare intellectually for a range of uncertain threats and scenarios. Since even with great planning and foresight we can't predict or influence all future events, Army leaders work to shape the future on terms they can control, using diplomatic, informational, military, and economic instruments of national power.

- *Uncertainty because even as we cope with information overload, we cannot be sure we have interpreted correctly—nor do we have the luxury of time.* Because the Army's top leaders are constantly involved in planning for the unexpected, there's a temptation to analyze things endlessly. There's always new information; there's always a reason to wait for the next batch of reports or the next dispatch. Strategic leaders' perspective, wisdom, courage, and sense of timing help them make decisions in the face of uncertainty.

- *Complexity because every event and every variable are embedded in a web of interconnecting factors.* The complexity of the Army leader's environment requires patience, the willingness to think before acting. Furthermore, the importance of conceptual and analytical skills increases as an organizational leader moves into positions of greater responsibility. Organizational environments with multiple dimensions offer problems that become more abstract, complex, and uncertain. The complex national security environment—the Army's leaders must deal competently with the executive branch, the legislature, the private sector at a minimum—requires an in-depth knowledge of the political, economic, informational, and military elements of national power as well as the interrelationships among them.

- *Ambiguity because change often brings paradox, as in the phrase, "Think globally, act locally."* Army leaders must be able to expand their frame of reference to fit a situation rather than reduce a situation to fit their preconceptions. They keep Army values and force capabilities in mind as they focus on national policy. Because of their maturity and wisdom, they tolerate ambiguity, knowing they will never have all the information they want. Instead, they carefully analyze events and decide when to make a decision, realizing that they must innovate and accept some risk.

In a VUCA environment, strategic leaders think in multiple time domains and operate flexibly to manage change. Strategic leaders deal with change by being proactive, not reactive. They anticipate change even as they shield their organizations from unimportant and bothersome influences; they use the change-drivers of technology, education, doctrine, equipment, and organization to control the direction and pace of change. Strategic leaders fight complexity by encompassing it. They must be more complex than the situations they face. Once they make decisions, strategic leaders then explain them to the Army and the nation, and in the process impose order on the uncertainty and ambiguity of the situation. Strategic leaders not only understand the environment themselves but also translate their understanding to others. Moreover, strategic leaders often collaborate with other leaders over whom they have minimal authority.

The VUCA environment we face today affects not only leaders at the strategic level but leaders at all levels. Actions by the Army's direct-level leaders—sergeants, warrant officers, lieutenants, and captains—can have organizational- and strategic-level implications. The Army's organizational and strategic leaders work to educate their direct leaders about the larger environment and the fact that small actions can have large repercussions. Exhibit 6.1 describes actions taken by leaders at various levels in a VUCA environment.

Regardless of the challenges we face in a rapidly changing world, the essence of leadership remains the same. The Army's basic definition of leadership is *influencing people—by providing purpose, direction, and motivation—while operating to accomplish the mission and improving the organization.* Without leaders an organization would be little more than a group of people whose random individual actions would cancel each other out. Leaders provide purpose, direction, and motivation to unite the efforts of people to achieve objectives. They convert the organization's human potential into coherent "action" aimed at achieving objectives, either to *fulfill the*

Exhibit 6.1. Action in a VUCA Environment

The 1994 U.S. intervention in Haiti (conducted under UN auspices) provides an example of strategic leaders achieving success in spite of VUCA, or volatility, uncertainty, complexity, and ambiguity. Prior to the order to enter Haiti, military leaders didn't know either D-day or the available forces. Neither did they know whether the operation would be an invitation (permissive entry), an invasion (forced entry), or something in between. To complicate the actual military execution, former President Jimmy Carter, retired General Colin Powell, and Senator Sam Nunn were negotiating with General Raoul Cedras, Commander in Chief of the Haitian armed forces, in the Haitian capital, even as paratroopers, ready for a combat jump, were inbound.

When Cedras agreed to hand over power, the mission of the inbound joint task force (JTF) changed from a forced to a permissive entry. The basis for the operation wound up being an "in-between" course of action inferred by the JTF staff during planning. The ability of the leaders involved to change their focus so dramatically and quickly provides an outstanding example of strategic flexibility during a crisis. The ability of the soldiers, sailors, airmen, and Marines of the JTF to execute the new mission on short notice is a credit to them and their leaders at all levels.

Source: Adapted from *Army Leadership.*

organization's purpose or to *improve the organization for its future competitiveness*. Action, by definition, involves change. Action involves moving the organization from the current state to some envisioned future state. Because of the infinite variability involved in "influencing people," leadership is primarily an art, an art in which leaders create "action" through the combined efforts of people in order to achieve objectives.

At high echelons, the character of the action that Army leaders create can be better described as "change." The term *change* better captures the nature of the action created by strategic leaders because of the qualitative differences in their environment. The time horizons are so great and the scope of the actions so broad that the term *action* fails to capture the magnitude of the effort, the difficulty involved in making an accurate assessment of the current situation, the uncertainty of creating a vision of the future, the complexity of building momentum and the level of commitment required to see it through. Strategic leaders create a vision of what's necessary, communicate it in a way that makes their intent clear, and vigorously execute it to achieve success. The Army is currently in the midst of major change initiatives that will involve change of doctrine, training, leader development, organizations, materiel, people, and facilities.

Leading Change

The Army has handled change well in the past. It will continue to do so in the future as long as Army leaders emphasize the constants—Army values, teamwork, and discipline—and help their people anticipate change by seeking always to improve. Army leaders explain, to the extent of their knowledge and in clear terms, what may happen, and how the organization can effectively react if it does. Change is inevitable; trying to avoid it is futile. The disciplined, cohesive organization rides out the tough times and will emerge even stronger than it started. Leadership, in a very real sense, includes managing change and making it work for the organization. To do that, leaders must know what to change and what not to change.

Strategic leaders must guide their organizations through eight stages if their initiatives for change are to make lasting progress. Skipping a step or moving forward prematurely subverts the process and compromises success. Strategic leaders (1) demonstrate a sense of urgency by showing not only the benefits of but the necessity for change. They (2) form guiding coalitions to work the process all the way from concept through implementation. With those groups they (3) develop a vision of the future and strategy for achieving it. Because change is most effective when members embrace it, strategic leaders (4) communicate the vision throughout the institution or organization, and then (5) empower subordinates at all levels for widespread, parallel efforts. They (6) plan for short-term successes to validate the programs and keep the vision credible and (7) consolidate those wins and produce further change. Finally, strategic leaders (8) maintain and reinforce the change until it permeates the culture of the organization. The result is an institution that constantly prepares for and helps shape the future environment. Strategic leaders seek to sustain the Army as that kind of institution.

Skills for Leading Change

Army leaders learn several skills for leading change.

Transformational Leadership

Army leaders leading major change initiatives are taught to use transformational leadership. The transformational style is most effective during periods that call for change or present new opportunities. It also works well when organizations face a crisis, instability, mediocrity, or disenchantment. As the name suggests, the transformational style "transforms" subordinates by challenging them to rise above their immediate needs and self-interests. The transformational style is developmental: it emphasizes individual growth (both professional and personal) and organizational enhancement. Key features of the transformational style include releasing the energy of and mentally stimulating subordinates; the leader considers them first as individuals and then as a group. To use the transformational style, a leader must have the courage to communicate his or her intent and then step back and give other team members room to work. The transformational style can seem risky initially because others are given great latitude in figuring out how to achieve the result. The power of this approach is often not appreciated until the result is within grasp or achieved.

Transformational leadership is best understood in contrast to transactional leadership. Transactional leadership focuses on the principle of exchange—rewards (or punishments) in exchange for the desired behavior (or the failure to behave as desired). Leaders who use the transactional approach usually are very directive, outlining all the conditions of task completion, the applicable rules and regulations, the benefits of success, and the consequences—to include possible disciplinary actions—of failure. They often apply "management by exception," focusing on their subordinates' failures, showing up only when something goes wrong. The leader who relies primarily on the transactional style evokes only short-term commitment from subordinates and discourages risk-taking and innovation, clear necessities for dealing with change and uncertainty. Using the transactional style alone can also deprive subordinates of opportunities to grow, because it leaves no room for honest mistakes.

The transformational leadership style allows leaders to take advantage of the skills and knowledge of experienced subordinates who may have better ideas on how to accomplish a mission. Leaders who use this style communicate reasons for their decisions or actions, and in the process, help subordinates develop a broader understanding and ability to exercise initiative and operate effectively. This approach produces the most enthusiastic and genuine response. Subordinates will be more committed, creative, and innovative. They will also be more likely to take calculated risks to accomplish the mission. However, not all situations lend themselves to the transformational leadership style. It may not be effective when subordinates are inexperienced, when the mission allows little deviation from accepted procedures, or when subordinates are not motivated.

Communication

Communication is an essential skill for leaders, as we saw in Chapter Three. It is also critical in leading change. People can only pull together in creating and implementing innovative change if their leaders clearly communicate where they are going. Leaders may have a clear vision for change, but it won't accomplish much if it is not effectively communicated throughout the entire organization. Army leaders constantly communicate the vision of Army transformation formally and informally, in speeches, workshops, task forces, written materials, and so on.

One of the main documents the Army uses to communicate its vision of change is "The Army Vision," a pamphlet that is widely distributed. This pamphlet clearly communicates the essential information that needs to go out in a change effort: why change is essential, the direction the organization is going in, and what will *not* change.

Communication at the strategic level is complicated by the wide array of staff, functional, and operational components interacting with each other and with external agencies. These complex relationships require change leaders to employ comprehensive communications skills as they represent their organizations. One of the most prominent differences between strategic leaders and leaders at other levels is the greater importance of symbolic communication. The example strategic leaders set, their decisions, and their actions have meaning beyond their immediate consequences to a much greater extent than those of direct and organizational leaders.

At the strategic level, communication becomes critical across boundaries. Change leaders in the Army know they need to serve as a bridge between the Army and others in society. They work to influence the opinions of those outside the Army and help them understand Army needs, and to interpret the outside environment for people on the inside, especially in the formulation of plans and policies. They focus on critical issues: What are the relationships among external organizations? What are the broad political and social systems in which the organization and the Army must operate? Because of the complex reporting and coordinating relationships, strategic leaders fully understand their roles, the boundaries of these roles, and the expectations of other departments and agencies. Understanding those interdependencies outside the Army helps strategic leaders bring effective leadership to the programs, systems, and people in the Army as well as provide leadership for the nation.

Of course, as we have already seen, communication is a two-way street, and includes listening as well as talking. Effective change leaders seek to listen, understand, and appreciate; they don't just deliver the message.

Mentoring

As we saw in Chapter Three, mentoring plays an important role in the Army. Past successes and failures can often be traced to how seriously those in charge took the challenge of developing future leaders. In the VUCA environment of the twenty-first century, the Army considers mentoring more critical than ever to develop leaders capable of responding to change. The success of the next generation of Army leaders depends on how well current leaders accept the responsibility of mentoring subordinates.

Honoring the Past

The Army has a history as old as our nation, a long and honorable past, and a mature, well-established culture—a shared set of values and assumptions that members hold about it. Army leaders recognize that they must honor the past even as they seek to shape the future. Indeed, honoring the past is part of the Army's culture. Military history is taught and great Army leaders from past wars are studied and honored.

By honoring the past, the Army's change leaders allow soldiers at all levels to realize that change does not dishonor the past, it builds on it. This permits everyone to more easily relinquish the practices and approaches that served their purpose in the past and to adopt new methods and strategies for the future.

Focusing on the Long Term

The Army perspective is that organizational change is institutional investment for the long haul, refining the practices of today for a better organization tomorrow. Improving the institution and organizations involves an ongoing trade-off between today and tomorrow. Wisdom and a refined frame of reference are tools to understand what improvement is and what change is needed. Knowing when and what to change is a constant challenge: What traditions should remain stable, and which long-standing methods need to evolve? Strategic leaders set the conditions for long-term success of the organization by developing their people, building the culture and teams required, and creating a learning environment.

In addition to demonstrating the flexibility required to handle competing demands, strategic leaders understand complex cause-and-effect relationships and anticipate the second- and third-order effects of their decisions throughout the organization. The highly volatile nature of the strategic environment may tempt them to concentrate on the short term, but strategic leaders don't allow the crisis of the moment to absorb them completely. They remain focused on their responsibility to shape an organization or policies that will perform successfully over the next ten to twenty years. Some second- and third-order effects are desirable; leaders can design and pursue actions to achieve them. For example, strategic leaders who continually deliver—through their actions—messages of trust to subordinates inspire trust in themselves. The third-order effect may be to enhance subordinates' initiative.

To strengthen morale and mobilize the entire Army to meet the challenges of change, its leaders cultivate a challenging, supportive, and respectful environment for soldiers and civilians to operate in. They simultaneously sustain the Army's culture, envision the future, convey that vision to a wide audience, and personally lead change. Strategic leaders look at the environment outside the Army today to understand the context for the institution's future role. They also use their knowledge of the current force to anchor their vision in reality.

Lessons for Civilian Organizations

Many lessons can be drawn from the Army's approach to leading change. The Army's use of transformational leadership and its approach to mentoring and communication are directly applicable to organizations in all sectors. Here we spotlight those aspects of Army leadership that we consider most crucial in leading change.

Harvard professor Rosabeth Moss Kanter—author of *The Change Masters* and *The Challenge of Organizational Change*—says that leaders and organizations that are successful at leading and managing change share three key attributes:

- *The imagination to innovate*. Effective change leaders help develop new ideas, models, strategies, and applications of technology that set an organization apart.

- *The professionalism to perform*. Successful leaders demonstrate personal and organizational competence, supported by workforce training and development, to execute flawlessly.

- *The openness to collaborate*. Leaders make connections with internal and external partners who can expand the organization's reach, enhance its offerings, or renovate its practices.

These abilities "reflect habits, not programs," Kanter says, "personal skills, behavior, and relationships. When they are deeply engrained in an organization, change is so natural that resistance is usually low. But lacking these organizational assets, leaders tend to react to change defensively and ineffectively."[3]

What Kanter calls "habits, personal skills, behavior, relationships," the Army sums up in three words, as we have seen: *Be, Know, Do*. The fact is, in our experience and the Army's, leading change in a powerful way requires doing so on the basis of a solid foundation: a bedrock of values, character, and competence that comes from good leadership at all levels. Programs, exhortations, slogans, and incentive systems will do little to bring about creative, systematic, adaptive change by themselves. Leaders of character and quality are key.

So the first lesson to draw from the Army's experience is that successful change is not possible without a basis of effective leadership and strong teamwork at all organizational levels. "Especially during the stress of change, leaders throughout the enterprise need to draw on reserves of energy, expertise, and, most of all, trust," says John Kotter. "Personnel problems often lurking beneath the surface of a team—all too easily ignored during placid times—come to the fore during times of change. The pressures of transformation make a strong team essential."[4] Leaders who are having difficulty in leading change, who are meeting resistance, or who seem to face repeated false starts need to stop for a moment and frankly assess the health of their organization and the quality of its leadership. Values, character, and competence need to be in place for a major change initiative to work well. As Kanter says, they need to be habits. And that means working seriously to develop the characteristics we have covered in the earlier chapters of this book: enduring values, character, climate and culture, teamwork, and leading from the front. There is no formula for change that allows any organization to skip these key steps.

Before embarking on a major change initiative, leaders should ask these questions of themselves and their organizations:

- Are our values clear and compelling?

- Do our leaders embody the mission, values, and beliefs of the organization—and do others clearly see them this way as well?

- Do we appreciate the worth and dignity of our people and treat them in a way that reflects this?

- What are our leadership strengths? What areas need to be strengthened?

- Is leadership development at all levels an ongoing priority and practice?

- Do we lead from the front? Do we anticipate change or simply react to crises?

- Have we developed real teams with people who put the team ahead of personal agendas?

- Do we communicate effectively and know that communication is not merely saying something but rather being heard?

Once the ground is prepared, there are specific tools and approaches that leaders can use to take charge of change and help others to do so as well. The Army emphasis on honoring the past could be profitably adopted by many companies today. Change often means letting go of structures, practices, and beliefs that no longer work—"planned abandonment," in Peter Drucker's phrase. But it matters greatly how past practices are abandoned. Unfortunately, leaders new to an organization often denigrate the accomplishments and values of their predecessors, a practice that reveals insecurity, not strength. We have all seen stories in the business press about new CEOs coming into a company vowing to sweep out "old, discredited" practices of their predecessors, not realizing the impact this has on employees or the resistance it provokes.

Not acknowledging and appreciating the past—what we used to be and perhaps still are—short-circuits a critical part of the change process, letting go. When facing major change, people need to be able to say good-bye to the past, according to William Bridges, author of *The Way of Transition*. "The first requirement [of change] is that people have to let go of the way that things—and, worse, the way that they themselves—used to be," Bridges says. "It isn't just a personal preference you are asking them to give up. You are asking them to let go of the way of engaging or accomplishing tasks that made them successful in the past. You are asking them to let go of what feels to them like their whole world of experience, their sense of identity, even 'reality' itself."[5] Honoring the past allows people to say good-bye more easily to the past and then turn to face the future.

The flip side of honoring the past for the Army is making a commitment to the future and taking a long-term view. Army leaders look ahead many years, with the perspective of an institution that is older than the U.S. Constitution. In contrast, many companies seem to follow the "flavor of the month," adopting various strategies, training methods, approaches that seem "hot" at the moment or that have been publicized in best-selling business books. Consistency and long-range focus are neglected in the press to demonstrate immediate results. Of course, the irony is that because these companies fail to look for long-term solutions, they move from short-term crisis to short-term crisis as though they were on a treadmill. Xerox, AT&T, Sears, and United Airlines are among the many companies that have experienced prolonged periods on the treadmill of crises.

We have recently witnessed the pernicious effect of this short-term focus among executives who were only concerned about meeting the expectations of Wall Street, propping up their stock price, and exercising their stock options or collecting their annual bonuses. These leaders placed their personal aggrandizement ahead of the good of their organization, sacrificing employees and shareholders alike. Leaders who focus excessively on short-term results do no favors for the organization.

In closing, we would remind leaders everywhere that just as we are responsible for understanding the organization's needs in a VUCA environment and leading the changes necessary to prepare it for the future, we must also assess our personal strengths and take responsibility for planning our own development in a rapidly changing world. Organizational and personal change go hand in hand, as the Army so rightly emphasizes. In meeting the challenges of change, each of us must look at the intensely personal challenges of our health, our well-being, our relationships with others, and the promptings of our spiritual life—however we define it—treating ourselves as whole human beings.

By definition, major change involves innovation. And Peter Drucker tells us that innovation is a discipline, not the inscrutable magic of genius. Innovation, he says, "is not being brilliant, it's being conscientious." Innovation is a key discipline for leaders of change.

BUILDING AND LEADING LEARNING ORGANIZATIONS

V Corps "Vipers"
Ready to Rock

By Sgt. Amy Abbott,
V Corps Public Affairs Office

CAMP VIRGINIA, Kuwait (Army News Service,
March 19, 2003)—"It's important that you stay
close together. I've said it 100 times, and here's 101:
'We ain't got no friendlies in front of us,'" said a
stern Staff Sgt. Wade Cherms.

The platoon of "Vipers" from B Company,
1st Battalion, 41st Infantry Regiment, Fort Riley,
Kansas, listens intently to the guidance of their squad
leader. As they sit in the sand, wiping off a day's
worth of tough training in the desert's sweltering heat,
they discuss what they did well, and what they can
improve next time.

The 2nd platoon soldiers, from the 3rd Brigade
Combat Team of V Corps' 1st Armored Division,
spent the day going through room- and trench-clearing
procedures. With a staged set made up of sandbags
and taped dividers, the soldiers cleared "bunkers" and
secured "hallways."

"Just like everything else we do—practice, practice, practice. It hones their skills," said Battalion Command Sgt. Maj. Charles Griffin. "Like anything else, if you get complacent you lose your edge."

During their After Action Review the Vipers discussed everything from switching out their lead men to moving through the course faster and fiercer. Cherms summed up the AAR by asking, "Did we all get some training out of this?!" The platoon's answer was a unanimous battle cry: "Hoo-ah!"

[http://www4.army.mil/ocpa/read.php?story_id_key=315]

The most notable trait of great leaders, certainly of great change leaders, is their quest for learning. They show an exceptional willingness to push themselves out of their own comfort zones, even after they have achieved a great deal. They continue to take risks, even when there is no obvious reason for them to do so. And they are open to people and ideas, even at a time in life when they might reasonably think— because of their successes—that they know everything. Often they are driven by goals or ideals that are bigger than what any individual can accomplish, and that gap is an engine pushing them toward continuous learning.

John P. Kotter, "Winning at Change,"
Leader to Leader, *Fall 1998, 10, pp. 32–33.*

Because change is constant, as we saw in the last chapter, the Army stresses continuous learning as a requirement in meeting the challenges of change. "For most men, the matter of learning is one of personal preference," General Omar N. Bradley once said. "But for Army [leaders], the obligation to learn, to grow in their profession, is clearly a public duty." According to Noel Tichy, "The most successful organizations are the ones that become teaching organizations from top to bottom—the ones in which people at all levels share information and learn from each other."[1]

Leaders promote learning in at least three ways: through their own learning on a personal level, by helping others in their units learn, and by shaping and contributing to an organizational culture that promotes learning.

On a personal level, continuous learning means improving interpersonal and technical skills through study and practice. It also means learning about the larger environment—mastering new technologies, studying other cultures, and staying aware of developments at home and abroad. On an organizational level, continuous learning means that teams, units, and organizations are acquiring new knowledge and putting it to use to improve practices, systems, and performance.

The Army takes both personal and organizational learning seriously and expects leaders at all levels to model the appropriate behavior. Army leaders model self-development for their people, because they are constantly learning themselves. Army leaders seek to educate and train themselves beyond what's offered in formal Army training or even in their assignments. And they realize they must remain flexible when trying to make sense of their experiences. The leader who works day after day after day and never stops to ask, "How can I do this better?" is not going to learn and won't improve the team or the organization. The Army encourages leaders to look at their experience and find better ways of doing things. Effective leaders aren't afraid to challenge "the way things are done around here." When the answer to "Why do we do it that way?" is only "Because we've always done it that way," it's time for a closer look. Teams that have found a way that works still may not be doing things the best way. Unless leaders are willing to question how things are, no one will ever know what can be. Rigid, lockstep thinking and plain mental laziness stifle learning. In the Army, effective leaders fight these personal habits by challenging themselves, using imagination, asking questions, and listening to others, including their subordinates.

Helping People Learn

Army leaders encourage their subordinates to learn and reward their self-development efforts. They design and integrate leader development programs into everyday training. They aim to capture learning in common duties, ensure timely feedback, and allow reflection and analysis. As Frederick the Great said, "What good is experience if you do not reflect?" Learning is continuous and occurs throughout an organization: someone is always experiencing something from which a lesson can be drawn. But if this learning isn't captured and spread to others, it's usefulness is limited. For this reason, Army leaders promote continual teaching at all levels; the organization as a whole shares knowledge and applies relevant lessons. They have systems in place—such as the Center for Army Lessons Learned—to collect and disseminate those lessons so that individual discoveries become organizational tools. This commitment improves organizational programs, processes, and performances.

The Army strives to develop and maintain the conditions that help people learn. Army leaders explain why learning is important and how it leads to better performance, so that people will be motivated to learn. They involve people in the learning process by making it active. Active engagement in learning makes it more meaningful and memorable. And they share experiences of their own learning.

Even at the top strategic level, Army leaders develop subordinates by sharing the benefit of their perspective and experience. People arriving at the Pentagon know how the Army works in the field, but regardless of what they may have read, they don't really know how the institutional Army works. Strategic leaders act as a kind of sponsor by introducing them to the important players and pointing out the important places and activities. Strategic leaders become mentors as they underwrite the learning, efforts, projects, and ideas of rising leaders. The moral responsibility associated with mentoring is compelling for all leaders; for strategic leaders, the potential significance is enormous. Mentoring by strategic leaders means giving the right people an intellectual boost so that they make the leap to operations and thinking at the highest levels. Strategic leaders aim not only to pass on knowledge but also to grow wisdom in those they mentor. (We discussed mentoring in Chapter Three.)

Organizational Climate and Learning

The nation expects military professionals as individuals and the Army as an institution to learn from the experience of others and apply that learning to understanding the present and preparing for the future. Such learning requires both individual and institutional commitments. Each military professional must be committed to self-development, part of which is studying military history and other disciplines related to military operations. The Army as an institution must be committed to conducting technical research, monitoring emerging threats, and developing leaders for the next generation. Strategic leaders, by their example and resourcing decisions, sustain the culture and policies that encourage both the individual and the Army to learn.

The Army strives every day to become more and more effective as a learning organization, one that harnesses the experience of its people and organizations to improve the way it does business. Based on their experiences, learning organizations adopt new techniques and procedures that get the job done more efficiently or effectively. Likewise, they discard techniques and procedures that have outlived their purpose.

To maintain the Army as a learning organization, leaders at all levels work to establish an organizational climate that rewards collective learning and to ensure that their unit learns from its experiences. Army leaders create an environment that supports people in their organizations learning from their own experiences and the experiences of others. How leaders react to failure and encourage success is critical to reaching excellence. Subordinates who feel they need to hide mistakes deprive others of valuable lessons. Organizational leaders set the tone for this honest sharing of experiences by acknowledging that not all experiences (even their own) are successful. They encourage subordinates to examine their experiences, and make it easy for them to share what they learn.

It takes courage to create a learning environment. When anyone tries new things or tries to do things in different ways, there are bound to be some mistakes. Leaders learn from their mistakes and the mistakes of others. They pick themselves and their team up, determine what went right and wrong, and continue the mission. There's no room for the "zero-defects" mentality in a learning organization. As we have seen, leaders willing to learn welcome new ways of looking at things, examine what's going well, and are not afraid to look at what's going poorly. When leaders stop receiving feedback from subordinates, it's a good indication that something is wrong. Leaders who hammer home the message, "There will be no mistakes," or lose their temper and "shoot the messenger" every time there's bad news, eventually find that people just stop telling them when things go wrong or suggesting how to make things go right. Eventually, they will have to confront some unpleasant surprises. Any time human beings work in a complex organization doing difficult jobs, often under pressure, there are going to be problems. Army leaders are taught to use those mistakes to figure out how to do things better and share what they have learned with other leaders in the organization, both peers and superiors.

That said, it is certainly true that all environments are not learning environments; a standard of "zero defects" is acceptable, if not mandatory, in some circumstances. An Army parachute rigger is charged with a zero-defect standard. If a rigger makes a mistake, a parachutist will die. Helicopter repairers live in a zero-defect environment as well. They can't allow aircraft to be mechanically unstable during flight. In these and similar work environments, safety concerns mandate this mentality. Of course, organizations and people make mistakes; mistakes are part of training and may be the price of taking action. In the Army, leaders are taught to make their intent clear and ensure their people understand the sorts of mistakes that are acceptable and those that are not.

Improving the institution and organizations involves an ongoing trade-off between today and tomorrow. Wisdom and a refined frame of reference are tools to understand what improvement is and what change is needed. Knowing when and what to change is a constant challenge: What traditions should remain stable, and which long-standing methods need to evolve? Army leaders set the conditions for long-term success of the organization by developing subordinates, leading change, building the culture and teams, and creating a learning environment.

The notion of the Army as a learning organization is epitomized by the After Action Review.

After Action Reviews and Learning

The After Action Review (AAR) is a powerful learning tool developed by the Army that has drawn wide attention from the corporate world. As defined by the Army, an AAR is a professional discussion of an event, focused on performance standards, that allows participants to discover for themselves what happened, why it happened, and how to sustain strengths and improve on weaknesses. AARs integrate learning and action to analyze performance and decisions at all levels. They create a non-hierarchical environment for inquiry and team learning. Clear ground rules promote candor, participant involvement, and a focus on objectives. Formal AARs are scheduled after each mission and can last a few hours; informal AARs are run consistently after other events, even if they are five-minute reviews to build on lessons learned.

The ability to lead an AAR is critical for Army leaders. Army leaders at all levels from squads and platoons to the highest strategic level use AARs to promote learning that improves performance. Indeed, in 1999, then Secretary of Defense William S. Cohen and General Henry H. Shelton, Chairman of the Joint Chiefs of Staff, presented the results of the Kosovo After Action Review to the Senate Armed Services Committee.

The AAR is a critical tool for the Army, which operates in a VUCA environment, as we discussed in the previous chapter. Combat engagements and collective training exercises are complex events where the causal connections between individual performance, weapon effectiveness, and mission outcomes are obscured by the uncertainty, confusion, and stress of battle. Thus, the answers to the questions, "How did the unit do? And what can we improve in the future?" may not be immediately obvious to the participants or to those who control and observe collective training exercises. To derive training value and organizational learning from these exercises requires detailed feedback to the unit on their individual and collective performance and their relation to combat outcomes. This is the purpose of the AAR.

AARs have gathered much interest in civilian organizations but are often misunderstood. "The Army's After Action Review is arguably one of the most successful organizational learning methods yet devised," organizational learning guru Peter Senge has stated. "Yet, most every corporate effort to graft this truly innovative practice into their culture has failed because, again and again, people reduce the living practice of AARs to a sterile technique."[2]

Why is the AAR so often misunderstood and misapplied in the corporate world? Colonel John O'Shea, director of Defense Education Affairs at the Reserve Officers Association of the United States, says the culprits are values and culture. "The answer may be that a fundamental shift in organizational culture must first occur to allow the process to take hold and develop. That cultural shift must allow for honest reflection on collective and individual performance with full participation by all members of the organization."

Colonel O'Shea traces the development of the AAR as a learning tool to the 1970s, when the Army was recovering from the demoralizing experience of the Vietnam War. "The evolution began with a collective acknowledgment by senior leaders that things had to change and those changes had to begin with honest and candid appraisals of training performance. With veracity came the ability to adjust the approach to training where true organizational learning could take place and the AAR process could develop." The AAR became a powerful learning tool in the Army, O'Shea says, because Army leaders were "willing to examine performance collectively, across all ranks. . . . Leaders and subordinates alike were willing to discuss, candidly and professionally, their units' performance." There can be no sacred cows: "Unless all elements of performance are examined, including decisions made by the leader, the AAR will not be effective."[3]

Principles of After Action Reviews

Because the underlying values and culture of an organization are so crucial, we discuss the After Action Review in its full dimensions, going beyond technique and how-to steps.

The AAR is a problem-solving process. The purpose of discussion is for participants to discover strengths and weaknesses, propose solutions, and adopt a course of action to correct problems. A well-conducted AAR provides candid insights into specific soldier, leader, and unit strengths and weaknesses from various perspectives; produces feedback and insight critical to battle-focused training; and generates ideas for improvements. It is a tool leaders, teams, and organizations can use to get maximum benefit from every mission or task. After Action Reviews have the following characteristics:

- *They are conducted during or immediately after an event.* This ensures that events are still fresh in the participants' minds and makes the lessons learned more immediate and compelling.

- *They focus on intended objectives, related to specific standards.* Clear standards and objectives are critical for an objective discussion of performance.

- *They focus on soldier, leader, and unit performance.* No areas are off-limits for discussion, including the leader's decisions and actions.

- *They involve all participants in the discussion.* Bringing in a wide variety of perspectives creates a fuller and more meaningful picture of what happened and why. Every participant's contribution is seen as important.

- *They use open-ended questions.* Discussion is not guided or shaped to reach any particular conclusion. Open-ended questions invite everyone to add his or her perspective.

- *They determine strengths and weaknesses.* Looking at both provides a balanced picture. Too often, people are tempted to criticize what went wrong and ignore what went right. If the discussion focuses solely on what went wrong, people aren't going to be open and honest.

- *They link performance to subsequent training.* The whole point of learning is to improve performance in the future.

AARs are component parts of almost all Army training exercises, but their usefulness extends far beyond training. In fact, the Army stresses that the AAR is one of the most effective techniques to use in a combat environment. An effective AAR takes little time, and leaders can conduct one almost anywhere consistent with unit security requirements. Conducting AARs helps overcome the steep learning curve that exists in a unit exposed to combat and helps the unit ensure that it does not repeat mistakes. It also helps the unit sustain strengths. By integrating training into combat operations and using tools such as AARs, leaders can dramatically increase their unit's chances for success on the battlefield.

Four principles underlie the Army's approach to AARs:

- Every individual can, and should, participate if he or she has an insight, observation, or question that will help the unit to identify and correct deficiencies or maintain strengths.

- After Action Reviews maximize training benefits and organizational learning by allowing soldiers, regardless of rank, to learn from each other.

- An AAR is not a critique. No one, regardless of rank, position, or strength of personality, has all the information or answers.

- An AAR does not grade success or failure. There are always weaknesses to improve and strengths to sustain.

Feedback compares the actual output of a process with the intended outcome. By focusing on the task's standards and by describing specific observations, leaders and soldiers identify strengths and weaknesses and together decide how to improve their performances. This shared learning improves task proficiency and promotes unit bonding and esprit de corps. Squad and platoon leaders will use the information to develop input for unit-training plans. The AAR is valuable regardless of branch, echelon, or training task.

Individuals benefit when the group learns together. The AAR is one tool good leaders use to help their organizations learn as a group. Because soldiers and leaders participating in an AAR actively discover what happened and why, they learn and remember more than they would from a critique alone. A critique only gives one viewpoint and frequently provides little opportunity for discussion of events by participants. Soldier observations and comments may not be encouraged. The climate of the critique, focusing only on what is wrong, prevents candid discussion of training events and stifles learning and team building.

Of course, AARs are not cure-alls for unit-training problems. Leaders must still make on-the-spot corrections and take responsibility for training their soldiers and units. However, AARs are a key part of the training process. The goal is to improve soldier, leader, and unit performance. The result is a more cohesive and proficient fighting force.

Types of After Action Reviews

All AARs follow the same general format, involve the exchange of ideas and observations, and focus on improving proficiency. How leaders conduct a particular AAR determines whether it is formal or informal. A formal AAR is resource-intensive and involves planning, coordination, and preparation of supporting training aids, the AAR site, and support personnel. Informal AARs (usually for soldier, crew, squad, and platoon training) require less preparation and planning.

Formal

Leaders plan formal AARs at the same time they finalize the near-term training plan (six to eight weeks before execution). Formal

AARs require more planning and preparation than informal AARs. They may require site reconnaissance and selection, coordination for training aids (terrain models, map blow-ups, and so on), and selection and training of observers and controllers (OCs).

Formal AARs are usually held at company level and above. An exception might be an AAR of crew, section, or small-unit performance after a platoon situational training exercise (STX). Squad and platoon AARs are held before the execution of formal company and higher-echelon AARs. This allows all levels of the unit to benefit from an AAR experience. It also provides OCs and leaders with observations and trends to address during the formal AAR.

During formal AARs, the AAR leader (unit leader or OC) focuses the discussion of events on training objectives. At the end, the leader reviews key points and issues identified (reinforcing learning that took place during the discussion) and once again focuses on training objectives.

Informal

Leaders usually conduct informal AARs for soldier and small-unit training at platoon level and below. At company and battalion levels, leaders may conduct informal AARs when resources for formal AARs, including time, are unavailable. Informal AARs follow the standard AAR format.

Leaders may use informal AARs as on-the-spot coaching tools while reviewing soldier and unit performances during training. For example, after destroying an enemy observation post (OP) during a movement to contact, a squad leader could conduct an informal AAR to make corrections and reinforce strengths. Using nothing more than pinecones to represent squad members, he and his soldiers could discuss the contact from start to finish. The squad could quickly:

- Evaluate their performance against the Army standard (or unit standard if there is no published Army standard)

- Identify their strengths and weaknesses

- Decide how to improve their performance when training continues

Informal AARs provide immediate feedback to soldiers, leaders, and units during training. Ideas and solutions the leader gathers during informal AARs can be immediately put to use as the unit continues its training. Also, during lower-echelon informal AARs, leaders often collect teaching points and trends they can use as discussion points during higher-echelon formal AARs.

Informal AARs maximize training value because all unit members are actively involved. They learn what to do, how to do it better, and the importance of the roles they play in unit-task accomplishment. They then know how to execute the task to standard.

The most significant difference between formal and informal AARs is that informal AARs require fewer training resources and few, if any, training aids. Although informal AARs may be part of the unit evaluation plan, they are more commonly conducted when the leader or OC feels the unit would benefit. Providing immediate feedback while the training is still fresh in soldiers' minds is a significant strength of informal AARs.

Conducting an After Action Review

Conducting an After Action Review is a straightforward process. All participants in the event to be reviewed are gathered together in a suitable location. A formal review may require projection equipment, poster pads, and other material. An informal review may require very little. Reviews usually follow a simple format: Introduction, Review of Objectives and Intent, Discussion of Recent Events (What Happened), Analysis of Key Issues (which in the Army always includes force protection or safety issues), and Concluding Summary.

Introduction

Participation is directly related to the atmosphere created during the introduction. The AAR leader should make a concerted effort to draw in and include soldiers who seem reluctant to participate. The following techniques can help the leader create an atmosphere conducive to maximum participation. The leader should:

- Enter the discussion only when necessary.

- Reinforce the fact that it is permissible to disagree.

- Focus on learning and encourage people to give honest opinions.

- Use open-ended and leading questions to guide the discussion of soldier, leader, and unit performance.

Review of Objectives and Intent

The AAR leader should review objectives for the training mission or missions the AAR will cover. He or she should also restate the tasks being reviewed as well as the conditions and standards for the tasks. If the review covers a war game or similar exercise, the commander restates the mission and its intent, using maps, operational graphics, terrain boards, and so on, Then, if necessary, the leader should guide the discussion to ensure everyone understands the plan and the commander's intent. Another technique is to have subordinate leaders restate the mission and discuss their commander's intent.

Discussion of Recent Events (What Happened)

The AAR leader now guides the review using a logical sequence of events to describe and discuss what happened. He should not ask yes or no questions, but encourage participation and guide discussion by using open-ended and leading questions. An open-ended question has no specific answer and allows the person answering to reply based on what was significant to him or her. Open-ended questions are also much less likely to put an individual on the defensive. This is more effective in finding out what happened.

Analysis of Key Issues

Leaders can organize the analysis discussion using one of these three approaches:

- *Following the chronological order of events.* This technique is logical, structured, and easy to understand. It follows the flow of action from start to finish and allows participants to see the effects of their actions on other people, units, and events. By covering actions in the order they took place, soldiers and leaders are better able to recall what happened.

- *Examining each of the relevant functions and systems.* In the Army, these are called Battlefield Operating Systems (BOS), which include intelligence; maneuver; fire support; mobility, countermobility, survivability; air defense; combat service support; and command and control. (In the private sector, elements corresponding to BOS could be marketing, product development, manufacturing, customer service, finance, and information systems.) By focusing on each system and discussing it across all phases of the action, participants can identify systemic strengths and weaknesses. This technique is particularly useful in training staff sections whose duties and responsibilities directly relate to one or more system. However, leaders using this technique must be careful not to lose sight of the big picture. They must not get into long discussions about systems that do not relate to mission accomplishment.

- *Focusing on key events, themes, and issues.* A key events discussion focuses on critical training events that directly support training objectives the chain of command identified before the exercise began. Keeping a tight focus on these events prevents the discussion from becoming sidetracked by issues that do not relate to training objectives. This technique is particularly effective when time is limited.

One of the strengths of the AAR format is its flexibility. The leader could use the chronological format to structure the discussion, and then, if a particular system seems to have critical issues that the group needs to address, follow that function across the entire exercise. Once that topic is exhausted, the AAR could resume the chronological format. Each technique will generate discussion and identify unit strengths, weaknesses, and training the unit needs to improve proficiency. However, the leader must remember to do the following:

- Be specific, avoiding generalizations.

- Be thorough.

- Do not dwell on issues unrelated to mission accomplishment.

- Focus on actions.

- Relate performance to the accomplishment of training objectives.

- Identify corrective action for areas of weakness.

- Continually summarize.

Discussion of Force Protection (Safety) Issues

Safety is every soldier's business and applies to everything a unit does in the field and in garrison. The Army teaches that safety should be specifically addressed in every AAR and discussed in detail when it has an impact on unit effectiveness or soldier health. The important thing is to treat safety precautions as integral parts of every operation.

Concluding Summary

During the summary, the AAR leader reviews and summarizes key points identified during the discussion. He should end the AAR on a positive note, linking conclusions to future training. He should then leave the immediate area to allow unit leaders and soldiers time to discuss the training in private.

Following Up

The real benefits of AARs come from taking the results and applying them to future operations and training. Leaders can use the information to assess performance and immediately retrain units in tasks where there is weakness. After Action Reviews are the dynamic link between task performance and execution to standard. They provide commanders a critical assessment tool to use to plan soldier, leader, and unit training. Through the professional and candid discussion of events, soldiers can compare their performance against the standard and identify specific ways to improve proficiency.

The After Action Review is a training and performance improvement method that has accumulated an impressive record of success at multiple levels of the Army and has become part of the Army's culture. In today's Army, AARs are just a regular part of how leaders do things.

Lessons for Civilian Organizations

The Army became an all-volunteer force thirty years ago. Of course, in today's knowledge organizations, as Peter Drucker has said, *everyone* is a volunteer. More and more *we* choose the organization—the cause—with which to affiliate; leaders of organizations compete for the hearts and minds of people who want to be engaged. The opportunity to learn and to contribute, research shows, is a powerful motivator today. Organizations need to become laboratories of learning in order to compete effectively in the global marketplace but also to attract the talent that they need.

As never before, leaders need to be both constant learners and effective teachers. As Bob Galvin, former chairman of Motorola, has said, "The development of leaders and of lifelong learners are so intertwined that they must be addressed together."

How do we learn and teach the stuff of leadership? How do we make the new technology our own, using every learning and teaching tool to give our organizations the educational edge the future requires? Much of what we will learn and teach, we will invent. How we will do it is still beyond the horizon, so we will learn to learn from one another, a practice that the Army has developed into an art form, especially with After Action Reviews. AARs provide an exchange of information, ideas, and innovation that can begin to address the unprecedented needs of today's world. It is the task of leaders to open themselves and their institutions to that flow of ideas.

Peter Senge, author of *The Fifth Discipline: The Art and Practice of the Learning Organization*, spoke about the importance of learning to an audience of military and civilian leaders at the Investment in America Forum, held in June 2000 at the National Defense University in Washington, D.C., sponsored by the U.S. Army, the Drucker Foundation (now the Leader to Leader Institute), and The Conference Board. "The Army has taken very seriously the idea that learning is much too important to leave to chance," Senge said. "Now, most corporations would say, 'Of course, we know that— here's our training budget.' It's not just your training budget." All too often, Senge maintained, corporate training budgets are spent on activities that look like schoolwork. Although formal training does have a role, most important learning occurs outside the classroom, in real life. It's important to make learning an integral part of our lives, weaving it into the fabric of day-to-day activities.

"Have you ever been to an Army After Action Review?" Senge asked. "Or visited the Army Center for Lessons Learned? It's quite interesting. All the corporate people I know who have done it come back shaking their heads and saying, 'No, we don't know how to do this—this is different.' In fact, most corporations spend precious little time on reflection—serious reflection, together, among the people who have to take action again. But this is precisely what the Army does and has done—it has created an infrastructure for learning.

"Creating an infrastructure for learning means, first, making it possible to integrate reflection and action. In the Army, people come together. They've got data. They've got history. They've got facilitators. They . . . leave rank outside the door, which is what usually impresses corporate people the most, to see a frontline soldier challenge a commanding officer and not get his head handed to him."[4]

Senge has worked with a number of organizations to create infrastructures for learning, including Shell, FedEx, and Harley-Davidson. Harley-Davidson has been using AARs at a number of its facilities for several years. Tim Savino, director of organizational development for Harley-Davidson in Milwaukee, says that the AAR process is "a way to institutionalize a reflective activity. There's nothing fancy about the AAR process, but having the discipline to do it is another matter."

According to Savino, Harley-Davidson has found that the greatest challenge in integrating the AAR process into regular company practice is encouraging openness among the people involved—something many employees are uncomfortable with. It can be intimidating for a worker to point out the shortcomings of a production process when an executive who planned or championed the process is in the room. Savino said that it takes a while for people to feel comfortable telling the truth about problems in the organization when that truth can come across as criticism. For AARs to be effective, he says, they need to be set up so that everyone understands that "it isn't an opportunity to point blame but to learn about what's working and what isn't."[5]

In other words, creating an infrastructure for learning "means that there must be a day-to-day, hour-by-hour effort to build a climate of real values," notes Senge. Values are important for creating trust, which we all need in order to share ideas, experiences, and learning freely.

As General Shinseki explained later at the same conference Senge addressed, "Trust drives our ability to be successful. But it wasn't until 1997 that the Army as an institution decided to codify what were individual articulations of what we meant by 'Army values.' And it's simple—there are only seven of them. We talk about loyalty. We talk about duty. We talk about respect. We talk about selfless service and honor, integrity and personal courage. So on the one hand, you say, 'OK, that's great, what does it mean?' And it is in the meaning that those things become important, because without an understanding and absorption of that throughout the force, the quality of trust is never quite good enough."

As we have emphasized throughout this book, values underlie every dimension of effective leadership. Our advice for leaders who want to develop a learning organization is not to try to adopt the AAR tool as a "sterile technique," to use Peter Senge's phrase. Rather, they should focus on the values that make learning possible: candor, open discussion, teamwork, the admission of ignorance or mistakes, and an optimistic belief that we can shape a better tomorrow. Organizations that encourage learning have a culture in which people naturally ask, "What did we learn this time? And what should we do differently next time?"

Conclusion

The Army's approach to leader development is powerful—and widely applicable to organizations and institutions other than the military. You may have initially questioned that statement. But we are confident that this discussion of the Army's principles and practices of leadership that enable its preeminence as a ground force—the *Be, Know, Do* of leadership—also applies to businesses, nonprofits, and government agencies. In whatever organization they pursue their careers, people are people, and quality leadership is quality leadership—effective across the broad spectrum of professions.

Quality leadership builds trust and confidence. A 2003 Gallup poll on Americans' confidence in major institutions indicated that 82 percent of those surveyed expressed a great deal or quite a lot of confidence in the top-rated institution—the military. In comparison, 22 percent expressed that level of confidence in "big business," ranked next to last. According to Gallup's Frank Newport, confidence levels in big business "have never been high" during the thirty years that Gallup has been conducting its poll.

There is a common language among the most effective leaders in public, private, and nonprofit institutions. It is the global language of leadership and management. Whether working with colonels and generals at the Pentagon, with executives from the world's largest businesses, or with the leaders of social organizations, the principles and values of leadership are universal. As organizations in all three sectors move beyond the old walls toward a new common ground and common good, our common leadership language encourages new alliances, new partnerships, and new understanding.

We have noted that leadership is essential, even in an archetypal command-and-control organization. In the stereotypical picture of the old military organization, a few people at the top gave commands, and everyone down the line saluted and did what he or she was told. But this old concept does not describe today's United States Army. In a new world that is more diverse, localized, and challenging, leadership has to be everyone's job. There is no alternative. The Army has long understood that there is no substitute for principled leadership. Thus, it makes leadership everyone's responsibility. The Army's slogan—*An Army of One*—was designed with that in mind.

Orders and commands don't plant the seeds of commitment; leadership does. Remember the Army concept of VUCA: volatility, uncertainty, complexity, and ambiguity. In today's worldwide VUCA environment, people need to do more than they are told; they need to participate actively and willingly. They need to be committed to achieving a common objective in a world that is volatile, uncertain, complex, and ambiguous.

We find different kinds of authority in today's organizations. In the old command-and-control organization where rank equaled authority—or in the traditional hierarchical organization struggling to transform the old structures and systems—power was simply the use of physical or economic force. For much of recorded history, unfortunately, organizations have used coercive power to control workers, with guards, physical punishment, even the threat of starvation. Force is still the predominant method used to control workers in much of the world today, and the operative word in those environments is *control*. The hearts and minds of the people in the organization are largely irrelevant as long as they follow directives. In an organization of the past, people were *cogs* in a machine.

Mission-focused, values-based, demographics-driven leadership based on a shared commitment to a set of values empowers the organization of the future. Such organizations are found in all three sectors. For example, religious organizations, universities, and social sector nonprofits are largely based on stated values. People work in these organizations for less pay—sometimes as volunteers—because they are committed to the mission, values, and vision of the organizations. To serve, missionaries may endure tremendous hardship thousands of miles away from the parent organization to advance the mission. Social activists may risk hardship and arrest in championing their cause. In mission-focused organizations, the quality and character of the leaders drive performance and produce results. In these organizations, a leader's strength comes from the willingness of people to be led in a team that disperses the responsibilities across its ranks. The Army is the quintessential mission-focused, values-based, demographics-driven organization.

Many organizations and businesses today have realized the power of shared values and have worked to become more values-based. Unfortunately, discussions about values in some organizations amount to little more than lip service. As we have seen, the Army is exemplary in making its values live—Army values catalyze its members' actions. As we saw in Chapter One, Dr. James Crupi has said, "The Army has a system of values that people in the corporate world would die for." As each chapter in this book has emphasized, values support every dimension of effective leadership. Leadership based on shared mission and values creates true commitment.

If one lesson from the Army's approach to leadership is most important, it is that leadership is primarily a matter of the quality and character of the leader. Incentives, bonuses, stock options, and other rewards for good behavior cannot take the place of principled leadership. If motivation in our organization is based on carrots and sticks, the organization is always at the mercy of those who can offer more or bigger carrots. And sticks can, at best, ensure compliance, but not commitment. If compliance is all we want, then perhaps we don't need leaders of character at every level. But if compliance is all we achieve, our organizations will certainly fail in a VUCA world.

Consider the actions you and your organization take that can build or destroy commitment. Do you put yourself ahead of the good of the company, even as you talk about mission and values and the worth and dignity of all your people? It is not hard for people to sense the contrast between language and behavior—after all, actions *do* speak louder than words. And we cannot expect people to be committed—truly committed—to the success of those whose vision does not extend much further than personal advancement. "In a world where the very best people are ultimately volunteers," Jim Collins asks, "why on earth should they give over their creative energies to advance the greater glory of a leader whose ambition is first and foremost self-centric? They shouldn't, and they don't."[1] Executives can buy the appearance of commitment by offering incentives and rewards, but such a transactional approach to leadership does not build strong organizations or create an effective team. In contrast, if leaders commit to the good of the whole and not themselves, they can build powerful commitment. A position can give you authority, but only when you love your people and are dedicated to their well-being more than to your own do you become a leader of character. A critical lesson to take from this book is that we need to treat everyone with the dignity and respect they deserve.

The Army realizes that a leader is not just a position on the organizational chart, but a person with mental, emotional, and physical dimensions. People who are serious about leading realize that it is their responsibility to develop themselves before they seek to lead and develop others. It starts with focusing on developing character and competence. The VUCA environment requires leaders who are self-aware and adaptive. Self-aware leaders understand their environment, assess their own capabilities, determine their own strengths, and actively work to improve.

The Army's job is to win our nation's wars. To fulfill this mission, it is critical that soldiers possess the will to win, the ability to persevere when things get tough, even when things appear hopeless. Let there be no doubt about it: Army leadership is the indispensable ingredient that inspires that will to win. Of course, business, government, and nonprofit organizations do not often face the prospect of ultimate sacrifice. Yet people in many of these organizations do experience debilitating stress and fear—often produced by their own organizations, often produced by executives who hide behind directives and policies, who do not communicate, and who do not listen—who, in short, do not provide leadership. This is a great waste of human potential. If leadership of quality and character can lead people to make the ultimate sacrifice when the stakes are at their highest, it can surely accomplish great deeds in civilian organizations.

The Army is a learning organization that has evolved together with the nation through societal changes, technological advances, and ever-changing international relations. Throughout our history, the Army has demonstrated enduring principles and qualities in its service to the nation—subordination to civilian authority, leadership of character and integrity, respect for human rights, and continual learning. Today, the Army is at the forefront of society in respecting and embracing diversity in every form.

Since before the birth of our nation—for over 228 years—the United States Army and the soldiers who are the Army have served the American people with vigilance, dedication, and selflessness in both peace and war. The Army has sustained our democracy from Lexington and Valley Forge to Gettysburg, from the beaches of Normandy to the mountains of Afghanistan, and through civil strife and political assassinations that have threatened our nation from within. The Army has always stood firm.

A country that not too long ago asked, "Where have all the heroes gone?" has discovered in the U.S. Army not one hero or a dozen, but hundreds demonstrating that in this democracy heroes are present and serving with great honor under incredibly difficult conditions. Quality, character, courage, and service above and beyond the call of duty describe those who have served our nation in Mogadishu, Bosnia, the Persian Gulf, Kosovo, Afghanistan, Iraq—around the world and within the borders of the continental United States, in peace as well as in war. These heroes, leaders of great courage, have names, faces, and stories that are made manifest to us by television, in newspapers, and through the Internet. Giants of quality, character, and achievement walk in Army boots.

There are millions of American families for whom Army tradition and culture are part of their own history; the integrity, character, and heroism of Army leaders have been a part of their lives for generations. Today, as we observe these leaders' actions and listen to their messages, many things have changed in the environment in which we operate. But the basic definition of leadership and its shorthand—*Be, Know, Do*—has not changed. It will not change. We spend our lives learning how to lead and teaching leadership to future generations because we know that the quality and the character of leaders determine performance and results.

In the challenging years that lie ahead, the familiar benchmarks, guideposts, and milestones will change as rapidly and explosively as the times, but the one constant at the center of the vortex will be the leader. The leaders of the future will not focus on the lessons of *how to do it*, with ledgers of "hows" balanced with "its" that dissolve in the ever-changing strategic environment. The leaders of the future will focus on *how to be*—how to develop quality, character, mindset, values, principles, and courage.

The *how to be* leader holds forth the vision of the organization's future in compelling ways that ignite the spark that builds an inclusive enterprise. The leader mobilizes people around the mission of the organization, making it a powerful force in times of uncertainty. Mobilizing people—whether soldiers or employees—around the mission generates a force that transforms the workplace into one in which people and teams can express themselves in their work and find significance beyond the task, as they manage for the mission. Through a consistent focus on mission, the *how to be* leader gives the dispersed and diverse leaders of the organization a clear sense of direction and the opportunity to find greater significance in their work.

Our times call us to move beyond the old walls and together find the courage to move forward. All the "how-tos" in the world won't work until the "how-to-bes" are defined, embraced by leaders, and embodied and demonstrated in every action, every communication, every leadership moment. Leaders at every level in every enterprise can empower others with leadership across the organization until we have leaders of character at every level, leading the organization and the community of the future. We do not know what lies ahead; yet, whatever the challenge, leaders will rise, finding the heart, the language, and the caring that embraces, sustains, and ensures success in the future—and the Army leads the way. The Army serves.

The Army performs missions today similar to those it has performed throughout our history. The places and the methods differ, but the qualities demanded of the Army are unchanged—an ethos of service to the nation, the readiness to fight and win wars, and a willingness to accomplish any mission the American people ask of us. As we transform the Army into a force that is strategically responsive and dominant across the full range of military operations, our role as servant to the nation remains clear.

American soldiers remain the centerpiece of our formation. Their character and our values are the threads from which we make whole cloth. Soldiers define our relationship with the American people—loyalty to the Constitution, the nation, and its citizens; commitment to service; professional excellence; and obedience to civilian authority. Soldiers accept hardship and danger, and sometimes injury and death, in pursuit of these ideals. For over 228 years, the American people have relied on the Army to protect and defend the Constitution and to guarantee their freedom, security, and interests.

Notes

Chapter 1

1. *Army Leadership* (FM22-100), para. 3-26.
2. [http://leadership.wharton.upenn.edu/l_change/Interviews/index.shtml]
3. James Crupi, personal communication with the authors, 2003.
4. Patrick Townsend and Joan Gebhardt, *Five-Star Leadership* (New York: Wiley, 1997), p. 32.
5. James M. Kouzes and Barry Z. Posner, LeadershipChallengeOnline: FAQs on the Leadership Challenge [http://media.wiley.com/assets/57/13/lc_jb_faqs.pdf] (2002).
6. Emmet John Hughes, *The Ordeal of Power: A Political Memoir of the Eisenhower Years* (New York: Atheneum, 1963), pp. 124–125.
7. John W. Gardner, *Excellence* (rev. ed.), (New York: Norton, 1984), pp. 135–136.
8. James M. Kouzes and Barry Z. Posner, LeadershipChallengeOnline: FAQs on the Leadership Challenge (2002).
9. James M. Kouzes and Barry Z. Posner, *The Leadership Challenge*, 3rd ed. (San Francisco: Jossey-Bass, 2002), p. 45.
10. *Army Leadership: Be, Know, Do* (Department of the Army, 1999), p. 1-14.
11. Sam Manoogian, "Maintaining Your Focus," *Leader to Leader*, Fall 2002, 26, p. 7.

12. *Army Leadership: Be, Know, Do* (Department of the Army, 1999), p. 1-17.

Chapter 2

1. *Army Leadership* (FM22-100), pp. 2–8.

2. John Kotter, "The Power of Feelings," *Leader to Leader*, Winter 2003, *27*, p. 29.

3. Martha Lagace, "How the U.S. Army Develops Leaders," *HBS Working Knowledge*, Apr. 7, 2003.

4. Anne Deering, Robert Dilts, and Julian Russel, *Alpha Leadership: Tools for Business Leaders Who Want More from Life* (West Sussex, Eng.: Wiley, 2002), p. 83.

5. Paul J. Kern, personal communication with the authors, 2003.

6. Carol Hymowitz, "CEOs Value Pragmatists with Broad, Positive Views," *Wall Street Journal Online*, Jan. 28, 2003 [http://online.wsj.com/article/0,,SB1043696373554243384,00.html].

7. John W. Gardner, *On Leadership* (New York: Free Press, 1990), pp. 51–52.

8. Daniel Goleman, "Leading Resonant Teams," *Leader to Leader*, Summer 2002, *25*, p. 25.

9. John W. Gardner, *On Leadership*, p. 48.

10. Noel M. Tichy with Eli B. Cohen, *The Leadership Engine: How Winning Companies Build Leaders at Every Level* (New York: Harper-Business, 1997), p. 11.

11. James M. Kouzes and Barry Z. Posner, *The Leadership Challenge*, 3rd ed. (San Francisco: Jossey-Bass, 2002), p. 14.

12. Dean Spitzer, "The Energizing Leader," *Leader to Leader*, Summer 2003, *29*, p. 24.

13. Dean Spitzer, "The Energizing Leader," p. 24.

14. Raymond V. Gilmartin, "Creating a Platform for Leadership," *Leader to Leader*, Fall 2003, *30*, p. 34.

15. Herb Kelleher, "A Culture of Commitment," *Leader to Leader*, Spring 1997, *4*, p. 24.

Chapter 3

1. Max De Pree, *Leadership Is an Art* (New York: Dell, 1989), p. 12.

2. *Army Leadership: Be, Know, Do* (Department of the Army, 1999), p. 3-1.

3. Jean-François Manzoni and Jean-Louis Barsoux, *The Set-Up-to-Fail Syndrome: How Good Managers Cause Great People to Fail* (Cambridge: Harvard Business School Press, 2002).

4. Lauren A. Cantlon and Robert P. Gandossy, "The Little Things That Develop Great Leadership," *Leader to Leader*, Summer 2003, *29*, p. 56.

5. John Kotter, "The Power of Feelings," *Leader to Leader*, Winter 2003, *27*, p. 29.

6. Lois J. Zachary, "Turbo-Charge Your Leadership Through Mentoring," *Leader to Leader*, Winter 2003, *27*, p. 15.

7. John Kotter, "The Power of Feelings," p. 27.

8. Edgar Schein, *Organizational Culture and Leadership* (San Francisco: Jossey-Bass, 1992), pp. 1, 5.

Chapter 4

1. Noel M. Tichy with Eli B. Cohen, *The Leadership Engine: How Winning Companies Build Leaders at Every Level* (New York: HarperBusiness, 1997).

2. Noel M. Tichy, "Getting the Power Equation Right," *Leader to Leader*, Summer 2003, *29*, pp. 29–31.

3. John W. Gardner, *Living, Leading, and the American Dream* (San Francisco: Jossey-Bass, 2003), p. 16.

4. John W. Gardner, *Living, Leading, and the American Dream*, p. 16.

5. James M. Kouzes and Barry Z. Posner, *The Leadership Challenge*, 3rd ed. (San Francisco: Jossey-Bass, 2002), p. 16.

6. *Army Leadership: Be, Know, Do* (Department of the Army, 1999), p. 6-5.

7. Noel M. Tichy, "Getting the Power Equation Right," *Leader to Leader*, Summer 2003, *29*, p. 30.

8. "Managing to Innovate," in Frances Hesselbein, Marshall Goldsmith, and Iain Somerville (eds.), *Leading for Innovation* (San Francisco: Jossey-Bass, 2002), p. 151.

Chapter 5

1. Master Sgt. Emma Krouser, "3rd ID Drives Toward Assault on Baghdad," Army News Service [www4.army.mil/ocpa/read.php?story_id_key=241], Mar. 27, 2003.

2. Larraine Segil, Marshall Goldsmith, and James Belasco (eds.), *Partnering* (New York: AMACOM, 2003), p. 78.

3. Larraine Segil, Marshall Goldsmith, and James Belasco (eds.), *Partnering*, pp. 82–83.

4. *Fast Company*, Dec. 1998, *20*, p. 228.

5. Patrick M. Lencioni, "The Trouble with Teamwork," *Leader to Leader*, Summer 2002, *29*, p. 35.

6. Noel M. Tichy, *The Cycle of Leadership: How Great Leaders Teach Their Companies to Win* (New York: HarperBusiness, 2002), p. 133.

7. Harvey Seifter and Peter Economy, *Leadership Ensemble: Lessons in Collaborative Management from the World-Famous Conductorless Orchestra* (New York: Owl Books, 2002).

8. James C. Collins and Jerry I. Porras, *Built to Last* (New York: HarperCollins, 1994).

Chapter 6

1. *Army Leadership: Be, Know, Do* (Department of the Army, 1999), p. 7-1.

2. *Army Leadership: Be, Know, Do* (Department of the Army, 1999), p. 7-1.

3. Rosabeth Moss Kanter, "The Enduring Skills of Change Leaders," *Leader to Leader*, Summer 1999, *13*.

4. John P. Kotter, "Winning at Change," *Leader to Leader*, Fall 1998, *10*.

5. William Bridges and Susan Mitchell, "Leading Transition: A New Model for Change," *Leader to Leader*, Spring 2000, *16*.

Chapter 7

1. Noel M. Tichy, "Getting the Power Equation Right," *Leader to Leader*, 29, p. 28.

2. "From Post-Mortem to Living Practice: An In-Depth Study of the Evolution of the After Action Review," Signet Consulting Group [http://www.signetconsulting.com/aarsum.html], n.d.

3. John O'Shea, "Leadership Training Concepts and Techniques: The After Action Review," *Concepts and Connections*, 7(1), Spring 1998.

4. John Head, *Innovative Public-Private Partnerships: The United States Army and the Private Sector* (New York: The Conference Board, 2001).

5. Ricci Graham, "Bikers Learn from the Army," *Knowledge Management*, Feb. 2001.

Conclusion

1. Frances Hesselbein, *Hesselbein on Leadership* (San Francisco: Jossey-Bass, 2002), pp. xvii–xviii.

Index